Conservation Concerns in Fashion Collections

Costume Society of America
Book Series

The Costume Society of America book series includes works on all subjects related to the history and future of fashion, dress, costume, appearance and adornment, including historical research, current issues, curatorial topics, contemporary design and construction practices, and conservation techniques. These books range from scholarly to more general interest and vary widely in format as well, from primarily textual to heavily illustrated. The series embraces a variety of specialties, including anthropology and cross-cultural studies, contemporary fashion issues, textiles, museums and exhibits, research methods, performance, and craft or fashion design.

Conservation Concerns in Fashion Collections

Caring for Problematic Twentieth-Century Textiles, Apparel, and Accessories

Kelly L. Reddy-Best and Margaret T. Ordoñez

The Kent State University Press ◼ Kent, Ohio

© 2022 by The Kent State University Press, Kent, Ohio 44242
All rights reserved

ISBN 978-1-60635-428-5
Manufactured in the United States of America

Cataloging information for this title is available at the Library of Congress.

26 25 24 23 22   5 4 3 2 1

Contents

Acknowledgments

The authors thank Harry Kimmel, communications director of the Drycleaners and Laundry Institute (DLI), for facilitating access to DLI archives and assisting with photography. He has been very supportive of this research effort. The many analysts of the DLI analysis department deserve special recognition for their insightful evaluations and reports of consumers' problems. Thanks also go to University of Rhode Island (URI) faculty Linda Welters; Susan Hannel; Martin Bide; and Pat Helms, Professor Emerita. Rita Hindle also provided insightful information about textile products. Martha W. Grimm shared her expertise in conserving paper dresses. We appreciate the assistance with the archival research from URI Historic Textile and Costume manager Susan Jerome, Iowa State University Textiles and Clothing Museum research associate Suzanne LeSar, Jacquie Dorrance Curator of Fashion Design at the Phoenix Art Museum Helen Jean, and Newbold Richardson and Virginia Vis from Costume & Textile Specialists. Thanks go to Carol T. Smith and Erin Holman for their editorial skills and Zoe Annis Perkins for sharing her textile conservation expertise. Our enduring appreciation goes to our husbands Brendan Reddy-Best and Alfred Ordoñez for their moral support and patience.

We appreciate the financial support received from Kelly's parents, Elizabeth and Donald Poorman; the Enhancement of Graduate Research Grant from the URI dean of the College of Human Science and Services; and the Donna R. Danielson Endowment, administered by Eulanda Sanders, department chair and Donna R. Danielson Professor in Textiles and Clothing, the Department of Apparel, Events, and Hospitality Management.

We are thankful for the photography assistance from the students working in Iowa State University's Textiles and Clothing Museum including Isaiah Sents, Ginger Stanciel, Angie Gaylah, Jessica Zuniga, and Brindy Arredondo.

I (Kelly) would also like to express my deepest appreciation for Margaret. Margaret served as my thesis advisor from 2007 to 2010 at the University of Rhode Island and continued to be a long-term mentor and collaborator. This book has been the greatest joy to write alongside Margaret, and I am always grateful for all of our interactions and the knowledge she has shared with me along the way. My career would not be where it is now without her support and encouragement. I hope that everyone can have an advisor, mentor, and long-term collaborator like Margaret!

Introduction

Caring for collections of twentieth-century apparel, accessory, and textile objects, with their continuous innovations, is an ever-growing challenge. Recognizing problematic fibers, dyes, finishes, and fabric and yarn constructions is essential in maintaining objects' appearance, minimizing deterioration, and isolating those that are potentially harmful to other objects. Although twentieth-century magazines, journals, and websites have provided information about problems, a compilation of potential difficulties for people who work with twentieth-century textile and apparel collections has not yet been published. Based on interviews with experts in the textile industry and reviews of many contemporary publications, this reference manual provides information on potentially unstable twentieth-century apparel, accessory, and textile objects in collections and their aging properties related to handling, cleaning, storing, and exhibiting them.

Twentieth-century publications used to create the chronologies include textile-science textbooks, commercial journals, conservation references, and bulletins from a trade association identified by a variety of names since its inception. On August 6, 1907, the National Association of Dyers and Cleaners was formed; then on January 1, 1947, the organization announced its name change to National Institute of Cleaning and Dyeing. In 1953, the institute again changed its name to National Institute of Drycleaning (NID), and in 1972, this group merged with the American Institute of Launderers to form International Fabricare Institute. The latest name change occurred in 2010 when it became Drycleaning and Laundry Institute International (DLI). It will be referred to hereafter as DLI except when citing twentieth-century primary sources.

In the late 1930s, DLI's International Garment Analysis Laboratory, originally called the Package Analysis Department, began offering a very popular service of analyzing problematic garments for the dry-cleaning industry. During the subsequent years, the laboratory has published warnings and information about textiles in variously named bulletins that included *Clothes Care Gazette, Fabricare News, Fashion and Fabric, Selling Sense, Textile Analysis Bulletin Service, Laundry Analysis Briefs Service, Fabric Facts,* and *Technical Bulletin.* The organization sometimes published multiple bulletins in one month, resulting in over 950 publications throughout the twentieth century. The authors reviewed all bulletins from 1918 through 1999 and documented the reported issues in a chronological format; these bulletins served as the major source of information for this manual.

How to Use the Manual

Within the manual, the materials are grouped into seven chapters based on categories: fibers, fabric constructions, printed components, coatings, adhesives, finishes, and plastics. Within each category are several subcategories. For example, *plastics* includes cellulose nitrate; cellulose acetate; polystyrene; polyurethane foam; and unspecified plastic buttons, beads, and sequin adornments. Each subcategory provides a brief historical overview and description of the material; methods of identification; and a summary of the problems the material experienced related to cleaning, storing, and exhibiting objects based on information reported in the literature and the interviewees' and authors' experiences. Images of fabrics, garments, and accessories focus on problematic materials and illuminate descriptions in the text. Following the summary of problems are recommendations for collection caretakers who have to identify potentially problematic objects and make decisions about handling, storing, cleaning, and exhibiting them. Storage and exhibition that does not encourage further degradation of a problematic material is addressed in each chapter. Finally, a chronology of problems for each subcategory provides collection handlers with the time frame of when the literature published reports of issues.

Textile and apparel collection caretakers can use the manual in several different ways. If they know an object's date and material, the caretakers can identify potential problems and review the recommendations for preventative and future treatment. These can be particularly helpful because some materials experienced problems only during specific time periods for a variety of reasons. The specific solvents listed to identify manufactured fibers do not pose health hazards and may be readily available. Additional solvents that dissolve these fibers can be accessed from chemical supply companies and used with fume hoods. In some instances, producers did not resolve all of the issues before a product went onto the market, so formulations changed over a period of time. During times of recession, manufacturers might have chosen substandard materials that did not perform well or changed components due to supply or environmental issues. Both of these situations left the customers dealing with the issues. Bonded-wool shoulder pads and interlinings are one example of the product developers' choosing inferior components. On its timeline, this product experienced problems only in the 1950s and 1990s; textile and apparel collection caretakers should be able to identify this product and make informed identification, treatment, and storage decisions. If caretakers do not know a material or date, they can compare their material to descriptions and images within the manual.

Some materials covered in the manual are particularly problematic; therefore, the authors suggest that caretakers conduct a survey of materials in their collections to identify and monitor these objects' condition on a regular basis. Doing this will help prevent damage to adjacent objects in the collection. Materials that probably need to be isolated include rubber objects, polyurethane- and urethane-coated fabrics, PVC-coated objects, rubber-coated rainwear, flocked fabrics (particularly those dated in the 1960s), cellulose nitrate and cellulose acetate ornaments and accessories, and polyurethane foam. Rubber-coated rainwear, bonded-wool shoulder pads and interlining, and cellulose nitrate and acetate cause such severe problems that owners may consider deaccessioning objects containing them. If these materials are present in collections, the authors suggest identifying them, reviewing their respective problems in the manual, and then determining appropriate treatment based on the collection's mission.

General Storage Guidelines for Textile and Apparel Collection Materials

Throughout the manual are recommendations for identifying, cleaning, storing, handling, and exhibiting textile and apparel materials in collections. We offer the following information as a general guide for setting and monitoring environmental factors, including light, temperature, and humidity; however, we strongly encourage caretakers to review information for each particular material to determine whether further precautions need to be taken. While these guidelines are suggested as the ideal, the authors recognize that the conditions may not be achievable in many institutions or small collections due to staffing, funding, and space. Following these basic principles along with those outlined in the treatment recommendations in subsequent chapters will allow for the best possible care for apparel and textile collections.

Light

Light damages fibers, dyes, and finishes, and the degradation cannot be reversed. The damage can be minimized, however, by selecting the safest types of lighting and controlling the amount of light and exposure time. Sunlight and fluorescent bulbs emit ultraviolet (UV) radiation, which is harmful to fibers, dyes, finishes, and other vulnerable materials. Direct sunlight should be avoided at all times. The move to LED lighting in museums and homes more safely illuminates textiles because of limited UV and heat emissions.

Five foot candles (50 lux) is the accepted maximum amount of light for exhibition of textile-related objects, and sometimes objects can be viewed successfully with less illumination. Exhibition lighting exposure time can be reduced with motion-sensor-controlled lighting. Storage areas also can have reduced lighting if objects are exposed to light. Illuminating separate areas in a storage room individually, turning lights off when no one is in a storage area, and having controls on a timer all help prevent unnecessary exposure.[1]

Climate

Maintaining a constant temperature and relative humidity within exhibition and storage spaces is important. Frequent, sudden, or drastic changes in the climate can damage textiles as fibers swell and contract. A number of chemical reactions are humidity dependent as is mold growth.[2] For the majority of cultural materials, the range of 45 to 55 percent relative humidity with an allowable drift of +/−5 percent, yielding a total annual range of 40 percent minimum to 60 percent maximum and a temperature range of 59 to 77°F is acceptable. Fluctuations must be minimized.[3]

General Guidelines for Managing Twentieth-Century Textile and Apparel Collections

Develop a collection plan or determine whether an existing plan addresses the following:

- Isolating potential donations and new accessions until they can be examined and vacuumed.
- Looking for problematic materials when considering potential donations. Consider the life expectancy of questionable materials and balance the availability and cost of proper storage against the value an object will add to the collection. Avoid acquiring objects that cannot be safely stored or might create unmanageable storage problems.
- Documenting the condition of accessions with written descriptions and photographs.

Establish and implement a preservation plan that addresses the following:

- Creating and identifying well-ventilated spaces to isolate objects that may be harmful to other objects. Consider the costs of providing suitable ventilation and isolation for problematic objects.
- Systematically examining objects in a collection to determine whether they contain or are composed of problematic materials; evaluate condition and isolate those identified with problems.[4]
- Regularly monitoring the condition of problematic objects.
- Staff and researchers wearing gloves when handling objects and components that are losing plasticizers (weeping or becoming tacky) or producing acidic secretions.
- Having written and photographic documentation of objects once degradation has started, along with documentation records of an object's original condition to provide a detailed context in case an object does not survive.

Develop a Deaccession Policy

According to the University of Alaska Museum of the North, deaccessioning refers to "the process used to remove permanently an object from the Museum's collection or to document the reasons for an involuntary removal." A number of organizations and institutions provide thorough policies for deaccessioning on their websites; we encourage readers to review these polices in detail as we only provide a brief summary of this topic.[5]

During the deaccessioning processes, museum boards, directors, curators, and deaccession committees must consider numerous and complicated issues that expand beyond the need to deaccession due to problematic or hazardous materials. For example, legal considerations of ownership and promises in prior donor agreements must be reviewed and considered. In some regions, abandoned property laws must be followed. Deaccessioning Indigenous objects requires special consideration. Ethical reasons not to deaccession objects include to honor personal interest, to please donors, or to generate operating income. Deaccessioning is also labor, time, and resource intensive; museum professionals need to consider the cost and benefit of carrying out deaccessioning processes. In sum, deaccessioning is a complex process, and going through this process with transparency and detailed documentation is of great importance to uphold collection-management integrity.

The University of Alaska Museum of the North offers a document in its Collections Management Policy that addresses deaccessioning and disposal method options. After the museum committee on deaccessioning reviews problematic materials and considers all of the factors, destruction is one possible option for objects that are harmful or hazardous. Of particular interest for deaccessioning degraded objects is this statement from the Collections Management Policy: "Prior to destruction, the object will be evaluated to ascertain whether it contains any hazardous materials. If any hazardous materials exist, the object will be destroyed in accordance with all federal or state laws and/or university environmental health and safety procedures."

Definition of Terms

The manual includes the following terms in multiple instances.

Abrasion resistance—"The rubbing or friction of fiber against fiber or fiber against other materials. Fibers with poor abrasion resistance break and splinter."[6]

Blooming—A white powder appearing on the surface of a plastic.[7]

Calendaring—"A mechanical finish achieved by pressing fabrics between a series of two or more rollers."[8]

Commercial wet cleaning—A garment-cleaning process that involves a commercial programmable front-loading washing machine and specialized detergents, although processes and equipment varied in the twentieth century; the time, temperature, and agitation levels can be adjusted depending on the type of fiber, fabric, or material.

Conservation wet cleaning—A controlled handwashing procedure performed on objects or materials using light agitation and low to medium water temperatures. Preferably an object should be laid flat during wet cleaning and moved or lifted by supporting it underneath, since fabrics are heavier wet than dry.

Crazing—Microscopic cracks or splits on the surface or interior of plastics.

Delusterant—Substances added to manufactured fibers during the production process to decrease the fiber's luster; titanium dioxide is used commonly.[9]

Dimensional stability—"The ability of a fiber or yarn to withstand shrinking or stretching."[10]

Disperse dyes—Originally developed for acetate but increasingly used on nylon, polyester, and other synthetics; subject to fume fading on acetate but not a problem on synthetics.[11]

Dry cleaning—A process using organic solvents rather than water to remove oily and greasy soils. Some solvents, from ethyl alcohol and acetone to petroleum solvents, can be used in an open tray or for spot cleaning in a well-ventilated room. They have low toxicity but are flammable. Commercial dry cleaners using perchloroethylene—a better cleaning agent—use a closed system because of increasing concerns and legislation over its being carcinogenic. Adding an emulsifying agent and water to an organic solvent (referred to as a *charged solvent*) helps remove water-soluble soils, but if contact with water would be harmful to a material, a charged solution should not be used. Each commercial dry cleaning machine usually has a tank of pure solvent to clean without water being present. Elastomers, adhesives, finishes, pigment prints, and coatings can be harmed by organic solvents.

Elasticity—"That property of a material by virtue of which it tends to recover its original size and shape immediately after removal of the force causing deformation."[12]

Fiber—The generic name for each of the different materials that constitute the basic building blocks for fabric.

Hand—The feel of a fabric.

Luster—"The amount of light reflected by a textile material."[13]

Manufactured fiber—Fibers that are "produced commercially through regeneration from natural materials or synthesized from chemicals."[14]

Natural fiber—A fiber derived from plants, animals, or minerals.

Modulus—"Refers to the fiber's initial resistance to the tensile force, before it breaks, and is a measure of fiber stiffness."[15]

Paillette—A small, thin, often circular piece of glittering metal or other material used for decorating a garment.

Plasticizer—An additive used in plastics to increase flexibility and softness.[16]

Sublime (*sublimation*)—Transformation of a solid into a vapor when heated.

Tensile strength—The "force required to break a material."[17]

Thermoplastic—"Polymer materials that soften and flow under the influence of heat."[18]

Vacuuming—A treatment to remove particulate soil and mold from the surface of objects.

Weeping—When a liquid forms on the surface of a material.[19]

1 Fibers

Commercially, the manufactured-fiber revolution began around 1910 with the first large-scale production of a manufactured fiber, later to be named rayon. The manufacture of fabrics containing paper in 1918 and the modification of glass into filaments in the thirties did not reflect the technological changes that were to come as much as DuPont's development of the first commercially produced synthetic fiber, nylon, in 1938. The invention of nylon, and its successful marketing, stimulated the synthesis of additional fibers.[1] Methods to identify fibers are included below although blends with other fibers and the presence of finishes can confuse identification. A list of selected fibers, the date of their appearance on the market, and their brand names are in the appendix.

Rayon Garments and Accessories

Starting in 1889, scientists produced several fibers to imitate silk, all of them marketed as "artificial" or "art" silk.[2] In 1924, the term *rayon* was assigned to all cellulose-based fibers: cellulose nitrate, cuprammonium, and viscose.[3] The introduction of acetate, a modification of cellulose successfully marketed as rayon filaments after World War II, added to the confusion. Finally, in 1953, the Federal Trade Commission (FTC) established separate categories for rayon (viscose and cuprammonium) and acetate.[4]

Full-scale commercial rayon production began in the United States in 1910 and initiated the manufactured-fiber revolution. Scientists produced rayon by modifying wood pulp and cotton linters. Manufacturers dissolved, filtered, and then extruded a cellulose solution through a spinneret into an acid bath where the cellulose regenerated and formed continuous filaments; this procedure describes the basic viscose process used to make viscose-rayon fibers. This type of rayon had low elasticity, low strength, and low abrasion resistance when wet. Despite its limitations, fashionable apparel incorporated the new fiber; until the mid-1920s, though, manufacturers blended or mixed it with other fibers to compensate for its lower strength and abrasion resistance.[5]

In 1926, the German company Bemberg began to make cuprammonium rayon, another type of regenerated cellulosic filament, in the United States. Soon other German companies followed suit, setting up US plants.[6] Manufacturers did not inform consumers which of the four types of "rayon" they were purchasing. Manufacturers of viscose, cuprammonium, and acetate filaments made improvements to these fibers, but the new high-wet-modulus rayons marketed in the 1960s reflected the greatest change in the fiber's wet strength.

Garment and home-furnishing manufacturers used viscose and high-wet-modulus rayon in a wide variety of products. The two types of rayon often were not distinguished on US labels, so consumers did not know which type they were purchasing. Likewise, collection caregivers will not know the difference unless a label or brand name provides that information. See the appendix for rayon brand names.[7]

Identification

Rayon burns quickly with a bright flame, leaving a feathery ash. After the flame is extinguished, an area remains hot and glows; this afterglow is a typical reaction of burning cellulose (wood, paper, textiles). Since rayon burns like all other cellulosic fibers, additional characteristics are needed for identification. It is the only cellulosic fiber in filament form, and a microscopic longitudinal view of viscose shows multiple lengthwise striations that are shadows of the irregular serrated edges of viscose filaments.[8] Bright rayon filaments will have no delusterant, while dull ones will have the little dark spots indicative of a delusterant. Cuprammonium has no striations but burns like other cellulosic fibers; it often is a finer filament than viscose. Distinguishing the second-generation rayons from viscose is difficult without equipment to measure strength.

Problems with Cleaning and Exhibiting Rayon Garments and Accessories

Bulletins reported professional wet cleaning, dry cleaning, and steaming problems throughout the twentieth century beginning in 1914. Viscose rayon's low strength, dimensional stability, and abrasion resistance when wet caused significant problems during treatments. Professional wet cleaning shrank, distorted, and stretched rayon garments. Fig. 1 illustrates a 1940s rayon-crepe dress that shrank significantly during wet cleaning. Fig. 2 depicts a close-up of the rayon yarns from the dress in Fig. 1 that shrank in both the length and width. Dry cleaning also distorted and changed the appearance of rayon-pile velvets.

Manufacturers applied sizing to rayon fabric to add body. Steaming shrank and distorted rayon garments with and without sizing. Professional wet cleaning also dissolved the sizing on rayon, leaving the fabric discolored and limp. Four bulletins in the 1980s and 1990s reported that professional wet cleaning and steaming caused dark stains due to sizing solubility.

Dull rayon yarns had less resistance to light damage than the bright forms of these materials. Light damage took place because the titanium dioxide used as the delustering pigment combined with oxygen, moisture, and ultraviolet light (UV) rays accelerating the production of hydrogen peroxide. The hydrogen peroxide attacked the ether linkages in the rayon cellulose chains and shortened the polymeric-chain length, lowering the tensile strength.[9]

Fig. 1. A 1940s rayon-crepe dress that shrank during wet cleaning. Photo taken by Susan Jerome. Courtesy of the University of Rhode Island (URI) Textile Conservation Collection.

Recommendations for Cleaning, Storing, Handling, and Exhibiting Rayon Garments and Accessories

- Examine yarn and fabric structures before conservation wet cleaning.
- Do not conservation wet clean rayon crepe, highly spun rayon yarns, or tightly woven rayon fabrics.
- Use low agitation and low temperatures when conservation wet cleaning rayon garments, and handle with extreme care to avoid distortion.
- Whether or not a garment exhibits dark stains, be cautious when choosing to conservation wet clean and steam because these treatments may cause or increase staining.
- Dry cleaning can remove oily soils, but steaming should be minimized afterward because moisture could cause fabric distortion and discoloration.
- Exhibit delustered-rayon fabrics at low-light levels.
- Rayon garments or accessories do not present a problem in storage, handling, or exhibition.

Fig. 2. Close-up of the rayon crepe that shrank during wet cleaning. Photo taken by Susan Jerome. Courtesy of URI Textile Conservation Collection.

Chronology of Cleaning and Exhibiting Problems for Rayon Garments and Accessories

1914—Moisture distorted rayon fabric.[10]

1922—Moisture reduced the strength of some rayon fabrics.[11]

1940—Rayon-pile fabrics shrank significantly when professionally wet cleaned and could not be restored by steam.[12]

1940—Professional wet cleaning significantly shrank rayon taffeta.[13]

1940s—Conservation wet cleaning shrank and distorted rayon crepe dress (Figs. 1 and 2).[14]

1942—Rayon fabric significantly stretched when submersed in water.[15]

1945—White rayon yellowed over time.[16]

1948—Professional wet cleaning dissolved rayon sizing and caused shrinkage.[17]

1949—Professional wet cleaning flattened and matted rayon-pile velvets.[18]

1958—Rayon velvets crushed easily.[19]

1960—Dry cleaning distorted and changed the appearance of rayon-velvet pile.[20]

1964—Sunlight damaged dull-rayon yarns.[21]

1987—Professional wet cleaning dissolved rayon sizing, causing dark shading.[22]

1988—Steaming redistributed rayon sizing, causing dark ring stains.[23]

1990—Rayon-pile fabrics distorted when wet.[24]

1992—Viscose rayon lost 30 to 50 percent of its strength when wet. It also shrank during professional wet cleaning.[25]

1996—Professional wet cleaning and dry cleaning dissolved rayon sizing, causing dark shading and limpness.[26]

Paper Garments and Accessories

In some products, paper replaced textile fibers during World War I due to fiber shortages. Japanese manufacturers used paper for wefts in silk ribbons, print cloth, shirts, and upholstery cloth. Some German trench uniforms had a mixture of paper with animal fibers, and manufacturers in Amsterdam used paper to produce men's suits.[27] Fashionable paper garments surfaced during the mid-1960s in nonwoven, disposable clothing such as the garment in Fig. 3. The composition of these paper garments varies, and most do not have fiber content on the packaging or any attached labels. Some, however, are made of "80 percent cellulose and 20 percent cotton"; "100 percent rayon"; "100 percent Avisco Rayon"; a PFR (paper for recycling) rayon; 95 percent rayon and 5 percent metalized polyester; Kaycel—"New Wonder Fabric," 93 percent cellulose, 7 percent nylon; a blend of polypropylene and viscose rayon; "Fibron"—polyurethane coating heat-pressed onto paper; and "Confil"—a wet-laid polyester and cellulose blend marketed under the brand name Disposables. Some paperlike dresses that followed the short-lived fashion were noncellulosic nonwovens: Tyvek, spunbonded polyethylene, and Remay, spunbonded polyester.[28] Nylon and polyester yarns positioned vertically or as a scrim in the paper of some dresses provided extra strength and produced a searsucker-like texture. Rarer knitted paper dresses had more flexibility than the nonwoven ones (Fig. 4). Japanese manufacturers used plied-paper yarns in the under-kimono in Figs. 5 and 6 as a protective layer under a kimono.

Fig. 3. "The Paper Dress," by Waste Basket Boutique of Asheville, NC; knitted paper dress and close-up of knit, Phoenix Art Museum, L109.2021.

Fig. 4. "The Paper Dress," by Waste Basket Boutique of Asheville, NC; package label, Phoenix Art Museum, L109.2021.

Identification

A small sample of textiles made of paper burns with the distinctive burning-paper smell and afterglow. The odor will be different if the cellulose is blended with other fibers, but an aftergow still will be present. Microscopically, the paper is a composite and will not look like cotton or manufactured filaments although both internal yarns or scrim are visible on both sides of the paper.

(*Left*) Fig. 5. Under-kimono made from plied-paper yarns. Photo taken by Susan Jerome. Courtesy of the URI Historic Textile and Costume Collection (URI HTCC), 2012.99.02.

(*Right*) Fig. 6. Close-up of plied-paper yarns in Fig. 4. Photo taken by Susan Jerome. Courtesy of URI HTCC, 2012.99.02.

Problems with Cleaning, Exhibiting, and Storing Paper Garments and Accessories

Paper used in garments disintegrated during professional wet cleaning. Fig. 7 illustrates color loss that resulted from abrasion along the center-front fold of a child's 1966 printed-paper dress.[29] Initial packaging and later storage caused wrinkling as in the shirt in Fig. 8. Since manufacturers intended these garments to be disposable, Drycleaning and Laundry Institute International publications did not report any cleaning problems for paper dresses.

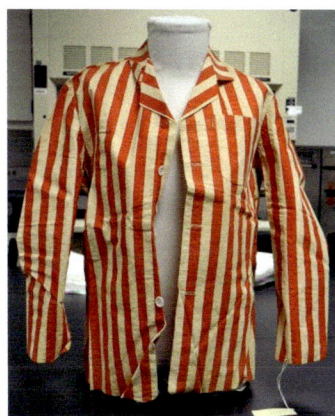

(*Left*) Fig. 7. Abrasion caused color loss on this 1966 child's printed-paper dress, especially along the center-front fold line. Courtesy of Iowa State University Textiles and Clothing Museum (ISU TCM), C107.

(*Above*) Fig. 8. Wrinkled circa 1960 paper shirt. Courtesy of ISU TCM, 2010.412.

Recommendations for Cleaning, Storing, Handling, and Exhibiting Paper Garments

- Do not dry clean or conservation wet clean garments if they contain paper components. Packaging sometimes specifies that consumers not put paper garments in a washing machine, which would result in a loss of fire retardant. Additionally, some papers, especially those of viscose rayon, would decompose.
- Do not steam. Some packaging warns against subjecting paper to a temperature higher than 70° F.
- Test an inconspicuous area of an object for its reaction to water; if the paper does not break into layers or printed designs are stable, humidify slight creases by sandwiching them between dampened blotter paper held in place by glass sheets.
- Reduce slight creases in three-dimensional parts of garments, such as sleeves and ruffles, by holding evenly damp blotter paper on the surface until humidity is increased sufficiently to relax the deformation.
- Reduce sharp creases and wrinkles by this method: mist the creases with distilled water; wait ten minutes and gently smooth the paper to flatten; cover with a dry cotton cloth and press the cloth with an up-and-down motion against the paper to ensure complete contact with no wrinkles; cover with glass plates, leaving no space between plates; allow several hours for it to dry, not lifting or moving the paper until dry. Discoloration in the paper resulting from ageing and tidelines are reduced with this treatment as the moisture moves into the cloth, although binder from the paper also can move. Repeating the treatment may be necessary to lessen long-set-in creases.
- Fold as few times as possible in storage to minimize creases; pad fold lines.
- Handle carefully and avoid abrasion to prevent color loss.
- Consider stiffness of fabrics and garments when choosing support methods for exhibition because the drapability of paper garments is different from garments made of other fabrics. Use caution in dressing and adjusting garments on mannequins to avoid stress and tears.

Chronology of Cleaning Problems for Paper

1918—Professional wet cleaning dissolved paper fibers incorporated in German uniform fabrics.[30]

1918—Professional wet cleaning dissolved paper fibers incorporated in some Japanese silk ribbons, print cloths, shirts, and upholstery cloth.[31]

1918—Professional wet cleaning dissolved paper fibers incorporated in some suit fabrics from Amsterdam.[32]

1920s—A Halloween paper costume lost its strength and color fastness when wetted.[33]

1929—In reseach comparing rag paper made of rayon to those made of cotton or linen, the test data indicated that "rayon is valueless in the rag stock for high-grade papers and may actually be detrimental to their quality."[34]

1960s—Wear and storage caused creases in paper shirt (Fig. 8).[35]

1960s—Paper garments stored in original packaging developed wrinkles and creases that are difficult to relax.[36]

1966—Color loss resulted from abrasion along the center-front fold of a child's printed-paper dress (Fig. 7).[37]

Acetate Garments and Accessories

The first commercial use of cellulose acetate as a plasticized lacquer was to coat the fabric wings of World War I airplanes. Following the war, the demand for acetate lacquer decreased, pushing manufacturers to research other markets for the product. Scientists developed a process that converted cellulose acetate into a filament with exceptional drapeability and high luster (unless delustered with pigments). Acetate was the first thermoplastic fiber, and with advances in dye technology it became commercially available in the late twenties. Fabrics of this new fiber exhibited many desirable silk-like characteristics; however, they had very low strength and were weaker wet than dry. Manufacturers used acetate for formal wear, linings for suits and coats, ribbons, graduation robes, and drapery and upholstery fabrics. They also created less expensive velvets by replacing expensive silk yarns with acetate.[38] Until mid-century, they often produced mixtures of acetate and rayon (rayon warp and acetate weft), and in 1958, the FTC categorized rayon and acetate as two separate generic fibers.

Identification

Acetate is very heat sensitive and can be identified by its solubility in acetone at room temperature. Acetone is available in small quantities as fingernail polish remover. The remains of a burned acetate yarn will be a hard bead since acetate is a thermoplastic fiber. Microscopically, a longitudinal view of a filament has lengthwise striations, but fewer than rayon. Bright acetate filaments will have no delusterant, while dull ones will have the little dark spots indicative of a delusterant.[39]

Problems with Cleaning, Exhibiting, and Storing Acetate

Acetate's inherently low strength, low melting point, and increased weakness when wet reduced its stability during cleaning. Agitation, moisture, and heat during both professional wet cleaning and dry cleaning distorted acetate fabrics. Wet cleaning permanently creased, delustered, shrank, and disfigured acetate.

Acetate's sensitivity to heat and moisture and susceptibility to color fading created challenges for consumers and cleaners. As a thermoplastic fiber, acetate softened or melted with the application of heat. Pressing melted acetate, causing glaze marks and permanently flattening acetate velvets. Some disperse dyes, developed to color acetate, discolored from exposure to nitrous oxide gases normally in the atmosphere or produced by burning coal, oil, or gas. The process is known as "fume fading," and gas-fading inhibitors added to the dyes provided only temporary protection. Garments hanging in storage faded most noticeably over the shoulder, down the length of sleeves, and in lengthwise streaks along the sides of skirts and trousers. Blue and red dyes are affected more than yellow dyes.[40] Figs. 9, 10, 11, and 12 illustrate three different colors of disperse dyes that fume faded.

(*Top left*) Fig. 9. Pleated acetate and nylon "Tubinyl" skirt by Koret of California from the late 1960s. Photo taken by Kelly L. Reddy-Best. Courtesy of URI HTCC, 1979.08.06.

(*Top right*) Fig. 10. Close-up of pleated dull-pink acetate and nylon skirt in Fig. 9 that turned yellow along both sides (see center of picture), due to air exposure while hanging in a closet with other garments. Photo taken by Kelly L. Reddy-Best. Courtesy of URI HTCC, 1979.08.06.

(*Bottom left*) Fig. 11. Blue-purple-acetate fabric sample fume faded along the fold-line crease, where the dye turned pink from exposure to the atmosphere while the fabric was stored in a stack of fabrics. Photo taken by Kelly L. Reddy-Best. Courtesy of URI Textile Science Collection.

(*Bottom right*) Fig. 12. The bottom of the blue dress changed color due to fume fading. Photo courtesy of Drycleaning and Laundry Institute International (DLI) (*TABS*, March 1994).

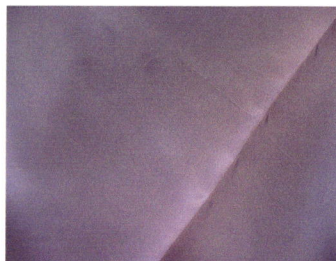

Recommendations for Cleaning, Storing, Handling, and Exhibiting Acetate Garments and Accessories

- Consider all cleaning options and consequences before implementing a treatment.
- Conservation wet clean acetate with minimal agitation and warm water; dry clean on a low-temperature cycle only if oily soils will be reduced by the solvent.
- Store acetate garments in boxes rather than hanging them in a closet to limit air exposure and avoid fume fading.
- Avoid covering part of an acetate object with a dust cover while the remaining sections are uncovered; fume fading will be greater on the exposed surfaces.
- When handling acetate velvets, do not put pressure on the fabric.
- Fold acetate velvets as few times as possible in storage to minimize creases; pad fold lines.
- Use cool temperatures when steaming acetate. When pressing, set the temperature at the acetate marking and then check the temperature in an inconspicuous place such as a seam allowance since acetate is especially heat sensitive because of its low melting point, and disperse dyes could sublime when heated.
- Steam acetate velvets on a needle board.
- Do not expose acetate fabrics to light for extended periods of time; lengthy exposure to light weakened acetate, especially when delustered.

Chronology of Cleaning and Exhibiting Problems for Acetate Garments and Accessories

1932—Applying too much heat to acetate caused glazed marks.[41]

1933—Any agitation while acetate velvet was damp crushed the pile.[42]

1939—Heat from steaming melted cellulose acetate.[43]

1950s—Acetate fabric fume faded in flat storage (Fig. 11).[44]

1958—Acetate velvet crushed and matted permanently with moisture and pressure.[45]

1958—Lengthy exposure to light weakened acetate fabrics, especially fabrics delustered with excessive amounts of pigments.[46]

1960s—Acetate and nylon skirt turned yellow along both sides that were exposed to air while hanging in a closet (Figs. 9 and 10).[47]

1962—Laundering acetate fabrics in hot water caused permanent creases and reduced luster.[48]

1964—Dull acetate yarns showed much less resistance to sunlight damage than did the bright forms of these materials.[49]

1964—Professional wet cleaning significantly changed dimensions of textured-acetate knits.[50]

1973—Dry cleaning relaxed pleats in some textured-acetate knit dresses.[51]

1975—Steaming permanently crushed and matted acetate velvet.[52]

1975—Minimal agitation during professional wet cleaning and dry cleaning permanently flattened acetate velvet.[53]

1976—Lengthy exposure to light weakened dulled acetate yarns.[54]

1981—Steaming permanently distorted acetate velvets.[55]

1988—Acetate fabrics had poor abrasion resistance.[56]

1990—Professional wet cleaning distorted acetate-velvet piles.[57]

1994—Disperse dyes fume faded (Fig. 12).[58]

1995—Disperse dyes fume faded.[59]

1997—Professional wet cleaning shrank woven-acetate garments as much as 5 percent and knits as much as 10 percent.[60]

1997—Moisture, heat, and pressure permanently flattened acetate velvets.[61]

Fabrics with Glass Filaments

Fig. 13. Tightly woven 1973 fiberglass fabric. Photo taken by Margaret T. Ordoñez. Courtesy of Margaret McWilliams. Swatch 22 in Joseph and Gieseking, *Illustrated Guide to Textiles*.

During the 1930s, the Owens-Corning Glass Company advanced glass-fiber production by extruding melted glass into long, fine filaments. The trademark name for the fibers was Fiberglas. Glass fibers had extremely low resiliency and extremely high breaking strength and modulus—the fibers' initial resistance to tensile force before they break.[62] Their extremely low abrasion resistance resulted in breakage along any crease. Except for special protective clothing, manufacturers did not use glass fibers for apparel. Typical end uses included draperies, curtains, window shades, and lampshades (Figs. 13 and 14).[63]

Identification

Glass filaments are stiffer than other fibers. They melt but do not burn, although a finish on them might burn. Microscopic examination is a good way to identify glass fibers. Under crossed polars (dark field) on a light microscope, fiberglass fibers disappear. Fractures on the ends of fibers will be conchoidal. If no binder or finish has been applied to the filaments, their surface will be smooth.

Fig. 14. Open-weave fiberglass fabric for window treatments. Photo taken by Margaret T. Ordoñez. Courtesy of Margaret T. Ordoñez's Sample Textile Collection.

Problems with Cleaning, Exhibiting, and Storing Fabrics with Glass Filaments

Bending fiberglass fabrics during handling, professional wet cleaning, and dry cleaning caused them to split and break. Over time, glass fibers broke, pulverized, and turned to powder. Filaments were very brittle, so movement caused breakage. The loose fiber fragments caused skin problems for handlers. For fiberglass fabrics with printed designs, see section on pigment prints at the beginning of chapter 3.

Recommendations for Cleaning, Storing, Handling, and Exhibiting Fabrics with Glass Filaments

- Vacuum carefully with a vacuum cleaner that has a HEPA filter. Dust and soil are easily removed from glass filaments.
- Conservation wet clean with minimal agitation and folding; do not dry clean.
- Wear long sleeves and nitrile gloves when handling.
- Handle with extreme care, and avoid bending and folding in storage and exhibition.
- Store flat with as few folds as possible to minimize breakage of filaments; pad fold lines.
- Steam will not reduce wrinkles.
- Be aware that degraded fiberglass fabrics can irritate skin and respiratory systems.

Chronology of Cleaning and Exhibiting Problems for Fabrics with Glass Filaments

1946—Glass fibers were brittle and eventually broke, becoming pulverized or powdery.[64]

1955—Folding split glass fabrics.[65]

1958—Fiberglass had a very low abrasion resistance.[66]

1958—Abrasion during professional wet cleaning and dry cleaning easily damaged glass fibers.[67]

1965—Professional wet cleaning shrank superfine-glass yarns.[68]

1992—Glass fragments caused skin abrasion on persons who came in direct contact with the object.[69]

1992—Glass fabrics had poor flexibility, which contributed to cracks and breaks.[70]

Nylon Garments and Accessories

In 1938, DuPont began commercially producing nylon, the first synthetic fiber. While nylon was extremely strong, it had a low modulus and stretched with a small amount of force. Nylon also was thermoplastic, allowing it to be heat set. Manufacturers made yarns in a wide variety of types from fine to coarse, and fabrics varied from soft to crisp, shiny to dull, and sheer to opaque, prompting their use in a wide range of products for apparel and the home.[71]

Identification

Nylon is soluble in a number of concentrated acids including formic acid. Without the presence of finishes, nylon melts before it burns and releases a celery-like smell, but the solubility test is more definitive. Microscopically, nylon without a delusterant is a clear, tubular filament; with a delusterant, the interior of the fiber has small dark spots, like other manufactured fibers. If the filament is trilobal, one or two longitudinal striations will be visible.[72]

Problems with Cleaning, Exhibiting, and Storing Nylon Garments and Accessories

Nylon garments and accessories exhibited a variety of problems. Some dyes in early nylon garments quickly faded when exposed to UV light. Nylon's thermoplasticity caused wrinkles to set in garments submersed in hot water. Over time and during professional wet cleaning, white nylon grayed and yellowed. Laundering also discolored nylon because it is a color scavenger, picking up unattached dye molecules from other fabrics in the wash water. Like later synthetics, nylon had an affinity for oil-borne stains. Light exposure weakened nylon. Also, nylon multifilament yarns snagged causing puckering in fabrics as a result of their inability to break. Although no care-related publications cautioned about static electricity, nylon's static generated under low relative-humidity conditions attracted dust from the surrounding environment, as with later synthetic hydrophobic fibers.

Recommendations for Cleaning, Storing, Handling, and Exhibiting Nylon Garments and Accessories

- Spot treat oily stains with a concentrated detergent solution before conservation wet cleaning; wet clean in a warm detergent solution to reduce soil and oil; if bleaching is necessary for discolored white nylon, treat with an alkaline hydrogen peroxide or sodium perborate solutions.
- Dry clean to reduce oily stains; oxidation of aged stains may limit removal.
- Avoid rubbing nylon garments against other garments, ornamentation, or rough surfaces to prevent snags, puckers, and static buildup.
- Keep surrounding surfaces dust-free when handling nylon garments and textiles.
- Be cautious when steaming; cool steam may not reduce wrinkling, but hot steam can cause uneven surface reactions.
- Store and exhibit nylon garments and accessories according to the fabric and garment construction; nylon fibers will not present problems.

1952—Steam at a temperature above 130°F shrank nylon fibers 15 percent.[73]

1955—Placing nylon fabrics in hot water set wrinkles.[74]

1955—Wax is not readily removed from nylon fabrics during professional wet cleaning.[75]

1958—Nylon grayed and yellowed with age.[76]

1964—Nylon yarns snagged and puckered fabrics as a result of nylon's high strength and inability to break.[77]

1972—Professional wet cleaning grayed, yellowed, and discolored nylon because it is a color scavenger.[78]

Casein-Based Garments and Accessories

The FTC designation for regenerated, naturally occurring protein fibers is *azlon*. Sources of the proteins for azlon include soybeans, peanuts, corn, cottonseeds, and milk. Although azlon products from peanuts and corn were produced in the twentieth century, the more successful and problematic were casein-based fabrics.[79] Chemists continued to experiment with casein and other azlon products during the century and into the twenty-first century, searching for environmentally friendly alternatives to less sustainable fibers.

An Italian chemist made filaments from regenerated casein that were marketed in 1936 as Lanital. In the United States, chemists with the Bureau of Dairy Industry of the US Department of Agriculture and the National Dairy Products Association also began experimentation to produce casein filaments. In 1939, Aralac, a regenerated casein, found a ready place in the apparel market due to war-related wool shortages.[80] First used to produce wool-felt and fur-felt hats, by mid-decade the soft, staple-length Aralac fibers blended with cotton, rayon, wool, and mohair in quilted linings and fabrics such as "gabardines, twills, flannels, serges, challis and fleeces, as well as in crisp, cool, summer-weight materials in apparel for men, women and children."[81] It dyed well, and its "almost white color lends itself to mixing with white wool in white or light felts" until 1948 when production ceased.[82] Fibrolane in Britain and Merinova in Italy continued to be produced until the sixties.[83]

Identification

An unmistakable way to identify casein-based fibers is to wet a small sample; it smells like sour milk when wet—one of the major consumer complaints during the forties. Since casein-based fibers were not strong enough to be used alone, their presence in a blend makes burning as a means of identification difficult. They do not contain sulfur as wool does so will not smell like wool burning unless the yarn being tested is a wool blend. Casein-based fibers are insoluble in dilute acids, hydrogen peroxide, and most organic solvents but are affected by alkalis. Microscopically, fibers are smooth with a circular or bean-shaped cross section.[84]

Problems with Cleaning, Exhibiting, and Storing Casein-Based Garments and Accessories

Casein-based fibers were weak, and fabrics lacked durability and wrinkled easily. When wet, they were very weak and produced a sour-milk smell. They were susceptible to microbiological growth and were degraded by some bacteria. Moths will not attack casein-based fibers like they do wool, but carpet beetles may. Although easy to dye, casein-based fabrics had poor colorfastness in washing.

Recommendations for Cleaning, Storing, Handling, and Exhibiting Casein-Based Garments and Accessories

- Do not wet casein-based fabrics, due to weakness and lack of colorfastness.
- Do not use a charged solution if dry cleaning to remove oily soil.
- Lightly steam casein-based fabrics to reduce wrinkles; hold the steam source at least 12 inches away from a fabric but do not allow a fabric to get very damp.
- Gently handle casein-based fabrics and store horizontally.
- Maintain a safe relative humidity to prevent biological attack.
- Isolate casein-based fabrics that have a sour-milk–like odor.
- Avoid stressing casein-based fabrics when adjusting garments on a mannequin.

Chronology of Cleaning and Exhibiting Problems for Casein-Based Garments and Accessories

1936 to the 1960s—The above section on problems with cleaning, exhibiting, and storing casein-based garments and accessories includes comments from numerous references, but none of them detailed a problem for a specific date.

Garments, Accessories, and Home Furnishings with Saran

The Dow Chemical Company introduced its trademark Saran fibers to the United States in 1941. The FTC also designated saran (at least 80 percent polyvinylidene chloride units) as a generic-fiber classification. Manufacturers included saran fibers in home furnishings, outdoor furniture, belts, shoes, sport bags, doll hair, and upholstery for public transportation due to their chemical and flame resistance. Polypropylene and acrylic later replaced the heavier and more expensive saran in those applications.[85]

Identification

Saran fibers shrink and melt when placed in a flame and are self extinguishing when removed from the flame. Saran fabrics are heavier than similar fabrics of other fiber contents.

Problems with Cleaning and Exhibiting Garments, Accessories, and Home Furnishings with Saran

Temperatures over 125°F caused shrinking, sticking, and permanent wrinkling. If heated, saran fabrics released acid, softened, and decomposed.

Recommendations for Cleaning, Storing, Handling, and Exhibiting Garments, Accessories, and Home Furnishings with Saran

- Use warm water temperatures in conservation wet cleaning to avoid softening and distorting.
- Do not steam or press fabrics containing saran.
- Handle, store, and mount garments, accessories, and home furnishings with saran according to the fabric construction; saran fibers will not present a problem.

Chronology of Exhibiting Problems for Garments, Accessories, and Home Furnishings with Saran

1946—Steaming excessively shrank saran.[86]
1958—Steam caused sticking, shrinking, and permanent wrinkling of saran fabrics.[87]
1970—Saran melted at a temperature above 125°F.[88]

Polyester Garments and Accessories

In 1951, DuPont introduced Dacron polyester to an eager US market; Eastman Chemical produced Kodel in 1958. Since then, scientists developed many variations. Fiber properties varied based on their chemical structure and the amount of drawing during manufacture. The consumer seldom was informed which variation a product contained.

Disperse dyes developed for acetates were the choice for dyeing polyesters, but manufacturers also used them for dyeing triacetate, nylon, modacrylic, and acrylic filaments and fabrics. Disperse dyes sublime—turn to a gas when heated. Polyester, similar to many synthetics, had an affinity for oil-borne stains. It had a wide range of uses in apparel and home furnishings; manufacturers often blended it with other fibers to take advantage of its durability and easy maintenance. Polyester with high-absorbency cotton produced a popular blend that also appeared in wrinkle-resistant fabrics. The market for polyester and polyester-blend fabrics for apparel and interior textiles grew every decade, and by the end of the century, polyester ranked first in use among fibers.[89]

Identification

Polyester is difficult to ignite and burns with a shiny, yellow-orange, sooty flame and sweet smell. It is self-extinguishing when the flame source is removed. The melted fiber is a hard bead. Polyester is resistant to weak acids, weak alkalis, bleach, and most organic solvents but degrades in strong alkalis, strong acids, and cresol. Microscopically, fibers are smooth, and their cross section can be circular, trilobal, or polygonal.[90] Pigment-printed polyester fabric can be identified by the pigment and binder sitting on the surface of the fabric and not being visible on the back side.

Problems with Cleaning and Exhibiting Polyester Garments and Accessories

Some early polyester fabrics lost dyes during professional wet cleaning and from inherent sublimation of disperse dyes. Agitation during professional wet cleaning removed printed pigments from polyester garments.

Recommendations for Cleaning, Storing, Handling, and Exhibiting Polyester Garments and Accessories

- Gently agitate pre-1980 polyester garments to avoid color loss when conservation wet cleaning.
- Dry clean to remove oily soils.

- Keep surrounding areas clean because the static electricity built up in polyester fabrics can attract dust and lint.
- Handle, store, and exhibit polyester garments and accessories according to the fabric construction, dyes, and pigments; polyester fibers will not present a problem.
- Use cool steam on colored or printed polyester to avoid sublimation of dyes from heat; hold the source of the steam at least 12 inches from the fabric to produce cool, wet steam.

Chronology of Cleaning and Exhibiting Problems for Polyester Garments and Accessories

1961—Rubbing readily removed pigment colors on multi-striped Dacron polyester fabrics while wet.[91]

1964—Many pigment-printed Dacron polyester fabrics lost color from abrasion.[92]

1976—Some disperse dyes in yarn-dyed polyesters sublimed.[93]

Acrylic Garments and Accessories

During the 1940s, fiber producers patented processes for spinning acrylic fibers. In 1950, DuPont marketed synthetic Orlon acrylic fibers. Within the next six years, manufacturers marketed Dynel, Acrilan, Verel, and Creslan acrylics. Produced by a variety of different processes, they had ranges of heat sensitivity, elasticity, and burning characteristics. Depending on the amount of drawing the fibers had undergone, acrylic fibers stretched rather easily. During manufacture, some synthetic fibers are drawn, or stretched, to align the polymers. Typical end uses for acrylics included woollike sweaters, suits, coats, fleece fabrics, blankets, and socks.[94] In 1968, fashion designer Pierre Cardin used Dynel fabrics, marketed as Cardine, to offer a collection of heat-molded dresses.[95]

Identification

Acrylic filaments are insoluble in most common organic solvents and are resistant to weak acids. All but Dynel and Verel melt and burn readily with a smoky flame and acid smell. The melted fiber is a hard bead. Dynel and Verel also melt but do not support combustion. Microscopically, their cross-sectional form can be dog bone, round, bean shaped, or lobed.[96]

Problems with Cleaning, Exhibiting, and Storing Acrylic Garments and Accessories

Lack of dimensional stability in acrylic fabrics caused some to shrink while others stretched. Bulletins during the 1950s and 1960s reported professional wet-cleaning and dry-cleaning treatments distorted and shrank acrylic garments. During the 1960s, a Kimlon-brand sweater permanently elongated after handwashing as seen in Figs. 15 and 16. Some acrylic garments had specially crimped filaments that caused fabrics to stretch out of shape if line-dried or hung vertically in storage.[97]

Steaming shrank, yellowed, and distorted acrylic fabrics including fleeces. High heat glazed, flattened, and fused acrylic fibers together. Steaming and heat often caused permanent elongation in fabrics that could not be blocked back to shape.

Fig. 15. Imported acrylic Kimlon by Miss Exquisite sweater that stretched permanently during cleaning. Courtesy of DLI (*Fabric Facts*, June 1963).

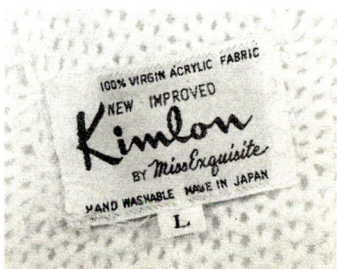

Fig. 16. Label from imported acrylic Kimlon by Miss Exquisite sweater, shown in Fig. 15, that stretched permanently during cleaning. Courtesy of DLI (*Fabric Facts*, June 1963).

Recommendations for Cleaning, Storing, Handling, and Exhibiting Acrylic Garments and Accessories

- Test acrylic garments in water for shrinkage or relaxation in an inconspicuous place before cleaning.
- If conservation wet cleaning is necessary, draw a template around the perimeter of a garment before wetting to block the size and shape before air-drying.
- Dry clean acrylic garments and accessories on a silk cycle to avoid high temperatures.
- Avoid hanging acrylic garments in storage to prevent elongation and stretching.
- Take extreme caution when steaming acrylic garments to avoid permanent deformation; use cool steam and hold the steam source at least 12 inches away from the surface to allow steam to cool; test in an inconspicuous place for yellowing or relaxation before steaming an entire garment.
- Handle and mount acrylic garments and accessories according to the fabric construction; except for static buildup, acrylic fibers will not present problems.

Chronology of Cleaning and Exhibiting Problems for Acrylic Garments and Accessories

1953—Professional wet cleaning significantly shrank Orlon-acrylic fleece.[98]

1953—Steaming shrank Orlon-acrylic fleece.[99]

1953—Steaming shrank and yellowed Orlon-acrylic fleece.[100]

1958—Finishing distorted Orlon acrylic (Fig. 17).[101]

1963—Professional wet cleaning and dry cleaning distorted acrylic garments (Figs. 15 and 16).[102]

1980—Stretching acrylic knit was permanent.[103]

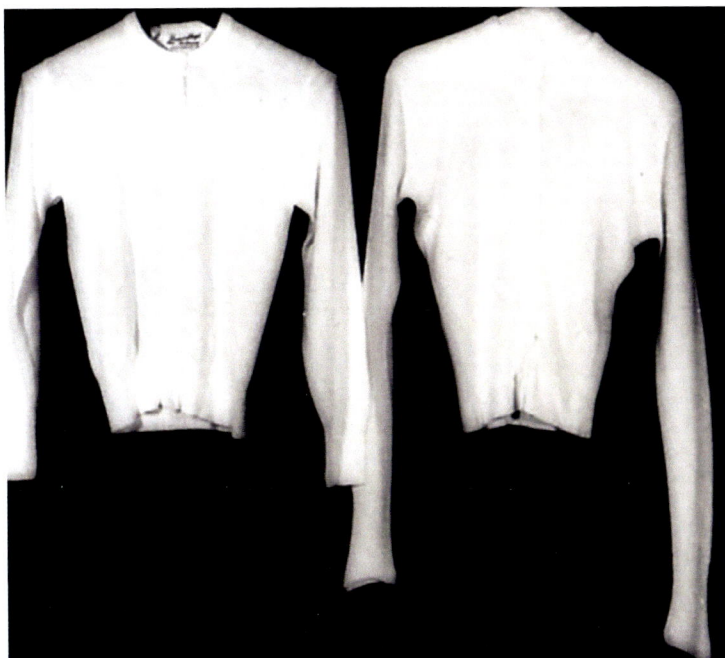

1991—Heat, steam, and tension caused acrylic yarns to elongate and distort permanently.[104]

1991—High heat flattened, glazed, and readily fused acrylic fibers together.[105]

Modacrylic Garments and Accessories

Union Carbide introduced Dynel modacrylic in 1951, and Eastman Chemical marketed Verel in 1956. The FTC classified it as an acrylic until a 1960 ruling created a separate generic category for modacrylic. This fiber was more heat-sensitive than the acrylic filaments developed in the 1950s. Modacrylic fibers were naturally flame resistant and had low strength; yet, elongation was somewhat higher than in acrylics. The major uses for modacrylic fibers included pile and fleece fabrics for apparel and blankets, draperies and curtains, wigs, and fake fur.[106]

Identification

Modacrylic fibers are fire resistant and self-extinguishing; they are soluble in warm acetone.[107] Microscopically, they have a dog-bone or irregular cross section.[108]

Problems with Cleaning and Exhibiting Modacrylic Garments and Accessories

Bulletins in the 1950s reported moisture- and heat-damaged modacrylic fleeces. Professional wet cleaning in hot water shrank modacrylic fleece, and steaming softened and permanently flattened it.

Recommendations for Cleaning, Storing, Handling, and Exhibiting Modacrylic Garments and Accessories

- Conservation wet clean or dry clean modacrylics but be aware of their heat sensitivity; avoid heated tumbling and steaming when dry cleaning fake-fur fabrics.
- Avoid folding and crushing fake-fur modacrylic garments and accessories; pad folds to reduce stress; the fiber is stable and should not create problems in storage.
- Be aware that steam and heat distort modacrylics. Hold the source of steam at least 12 inches from a modacrylic fabric so steam will be cool; if pressing, set temperature at coolest setting.
- Let the fabric and garment construction be the guides for dressing mannequins; modacrylic fibers will not present a problem.

Chronology of Cleaning and Exhibiting Problems for Modacrylic Garments and Accessories

1953—Professional wet cleaning significantly shrank Dynel modacrylic fleece after one treatment.[109]

1953—Steaming and brushing Dynel modacrylic fleece permanently flattened the nap.[110]

1955—Steam softened and permanently flattened Dynel modacrylic fleece fibers.[111]

Garments and Accessories with Rubber Components

Beginning in the nineteenth century, manufacturers produced natural rubber, from rubber plants, for clothing and shoes. For clothing, thin films of cross-linked rubber split into fine filaments provided elasticity. Synthetic rubber fibers (Lastex) marketed in the early 1930s had superior elastic properties and greater durability than natural rubber. Use of rubber filaments in garments faded with the introduction of spandex in 1959.[112]

Since the nineteenth century, garment manufacturers cut strips from sheets of natural rubber, but in the twenties, U.S. Rubber developed a method to extrude rubber filaments. The strips and filaments were used alone, as in the waistband of the trousers in Fig. 18, but the filaments could be covered by yarn in elastic bands and stretch materials. Wrapping a rubber filament with fibers or yarns created rubber-core yarns. When stretched, the cotton covering expanded in a coiled manner. The yarns appeared in stretch knits and woven fabrics. Rubber's advantages included low cost, "high stretch, elasticity, flexibility, good strength, and non-absorbency." Disadvantages were its low resistance to perspiration, sunlight, oil, oxidizing bleach, chlorinated swimming pools, and dry-cleaning solvents. It also deteriorated with age and at temperatures above 200° F.[113]

Identification

By the twenty-first century, rubber components might have lost all their elasticity and flexibility. They could be hard or brittle; some discoloration or odor might be associated with the degradation process.

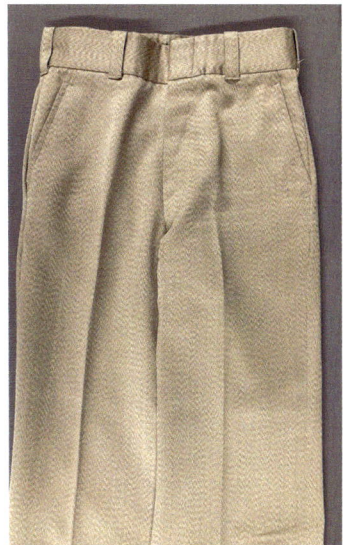

Fig. 18. Pants circa 1970 with gripper waistband made with strips of rubber to keep shirts tucked in. Photo taken by Susan Jerome. Courtesy of URI HTCC, 2002.12.01.

Problems with Cleaning, Exhibiting, and Storing Garments and Accessories with Rubber Components

Dry cleaning softened, decomposed, bubbled, blistered, peeled, shrank, and swelled rubber (Fig. 19). Components developed tackiness and reduced elasticity. Dry cleaners often replaced degraded gripper waistbands inside men's pants; however, once spandex was introduced in 1959, most dry cleaners stopped replacing the bands.

Rubber deteriorated over time. The core of wrapped yarns degraded and formed broken, hard pieces or a powdery substance with a peculiar odor. During wear, the yarns lost their elasticity and permanently elongated, resulting in a sagging fabric. Over time, elastic bands discolored, yellowed, and stiffened. Fibers released a gas that combined with atmospheric gases to discolor adjacent fabrics.

Fig. 19. Discolored, decomposed rubber strips in gripper waistband from pants in Fig. 18. Photo taken by Susan Jerome. Courtesy of URI HTCC, 2002.12.01.

Recommendations for Cleaning, Storing, Handling, and Exhibiting Garments and Accessories with Rubber Components

- Do not conservation wet clean or dry clean garments with rubber elastic bands.
- Isolate rubber-containing garments in storage to avoid damage to nearby garments due to off-gassing or tackiness.
- Consider that rubber components most likely will be brittle; handle with care.
- Do not steam rubber components of garments.
- When dressing a mannequin, be aware that the hardened rubber can be abrasive to adjacent-fabric surfaces.

- Avoid stretching fabrics with rubber components that have lost all of their elasticity; find ways to exhibit garments and accessories without extending rubber components.

Chronology of Cleaning, Exhibiting, and Storing Problems for Garments and Accessories with Rubber Components

1955—Dry cleaning increased tackiness of men's gripper waistbands in trousers.[114]

1958—Rubber-core yarns, wrapped in cotton, relaxed in areas stretched by wear, resulting in a distorted appearance (Fig. 20).[115]

1958—Dry cleaning, aging, and wear caused gripper waistbands to soften and become sticky (Fig. 21).[116]

1969—Dry cleaning shrank and deteriorated rubber-core yarns.[117]

1970s—Dry cleaning discolored and decomposed rubber strips in pants' griper waistband (Figs. 18 and 19).[118]

1970s—Red vinyl shoes worn in the seventies with imitation cork heels of brown molded rubber had been stored in an archival box since 1983; a 2003 inspection revealed that the soles showed some degradation and separation from the uppers; by 2007 the soles "had literally crumbled into pieces, highlighting the rapidity of deterioration and the need for prompt intervention in terms of monitoring and storage."[119]

1976—Rubber deteriorated over time.[120]

1976—Rubber-core yarns, wrapped in cotton, relaxed in areas stretched by wear.[121]

1982—Rubber-elastic materials lost elasticity after dry cleaning.[122]

1983—Rubber-core yarns deteriorated with age and broke down into a powdery substance with a distinct odor.[123]

1983—Dry cleaning swelled and broke rubber-core yarns.[124]

1988—Rubber oxidized and deteriorated over time.[125]

1988—Rubber became sticky, softened, stiffened, cracked, and liquefied over time.[126]

1989—Dry cleaning softened, separated, peeled, bubbled, and blistered rubber.[127]

1989—Elastic rubber waistbands deteriorated with age, releasing a gas and discoloring adjacent fabrics.[128]

1989—Dry cleaning swelled and deteriorated rubber used in cuffs and waistbands.[129]

1989—Dry cleaning softened, separated, peeled, bubbled, and blistered certain types of rubber.[130]

1989—Rubber deteriorated, yellowed, and released a gas that combined with atmospheric fumes and discolored neighboring fabrics.[131]

1990—Elastic bands decomposed over time and released a gas that discolored adjacent fabrics.[132]

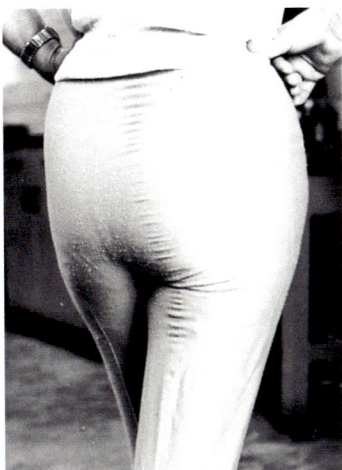

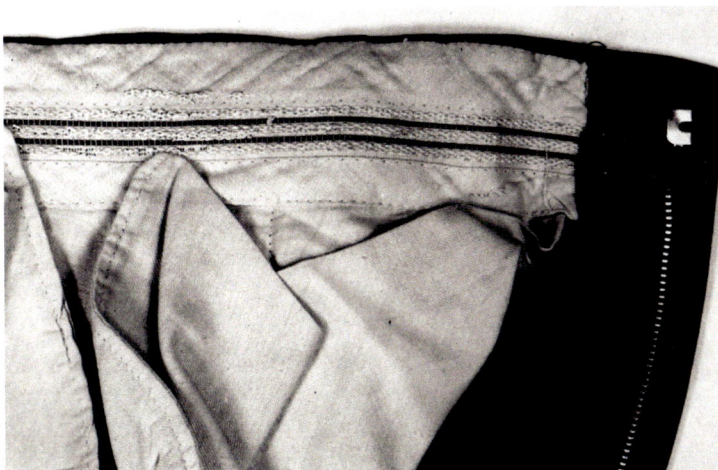

1992—Rubber space suits yellowed, oxidized, hardened, and disintegrated over time.[133]

1993—Elastic bands yellowed, decomposed, and released gases that combined with atmospheric gases and stained adjacent fabrics.[134]

Garments and Accessories with Spandex

US commercial spandex production began in 1959 and was introduced to the public soon after. Spandex, a urethane polymer, was an alternative to latex-based rubber and the first commercially successful synthetic-elastomeric fiber. It had excellent elasticity, defined as near instantaneous recovery. With high elongation, spandex filaments stretched 500 to 600 percent without breaking and returned to their original shape. In the 1960s, core-wrapped Lycra yarns appeared in girdles, brassieres, and swimwear (Fig. 22). By the seventies, the next popular use was in athletic wear. Designers such as Donna Karan featured garments made with Lycra, and DuPont had trouble meeting the worldwide demand. By the end of the century, all clothing categories included an increasing amount of spandex.[135]

Identification

Spandex filaments originally had extreme elasicity but stiffen and become brittle with age. Urethane burns with a bright flame and little smoke.[136]

Problems with Cleaning, Exhibiting, and Storing Garments and Accessories with Spandex

Garments that contain spandex from the last half of the century are losing their ability to return to their original shape after being

(*Left*) Fig. 20. Stretch pants made rubber-core yarns, wrapped in cotton. The yarns relaxed in areas stretched by wear, resulting in a distorted appearance. Courtesy of DLI (Lyle, *Focus on Fabrics*, 487).

(*Right*) Fig. 21. Pants with gripper waistband made with strips of rubber to keep shirts tucked in. Dry cleaning, aging, and wear caused waistbands to soften and become sticky. The cotton pocket is sticking to the softened rubber. Courtesy of DLI (Lyle, *Focus on Fabrics*, 510).

Fig. 22. Spandex core wrapped with nylon yarns in a 1973 raschel-knit power-stretch fabric. Photo taken by Margaret T. Ordoñez. Courtesy of Margaret McWilliams. Swatch 69 in Joseph and Gieseking, *Illustrated Guide to Textiles*.

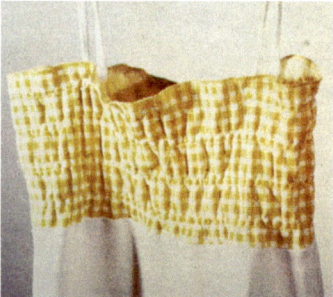

Fig. 23. Smocked camisole that lost elasticity during dry cleaning. Courtesy of Drycleaning and Laundry Institute International (DLI) (*TABS*, 1982).

(*Above*) Fig. 24. A 1970s Miss Hawaii cotton bathing suit with spandex band around hem of inner shorts. Photo taken by Kelly L. Reddy-Best. Courtesy of URI HTCC, 1994.07.18.

(*Right*) Fig. 25. Close-up of permanently deformed spandex band around leg hem. Photo taken by Kelly L. Reddy-Best. Courtesy of URI HTCC, 994.07.18.

stretched. Fig. 23 illustrates loss of elasticity in the smocked area of a bodice after dry cleaning.

Degradation of spandex began the moment the polymer was created. Spandex has a limited lifespan, with breakdown showing in the loss of recovery after extension. This means that 1960s corsets and similar garments shaped by spandex will not retain their integrity if stretched and expanded to dress a mannequin. Post-1960 swimwear is particularly vulnerable because chlorine in swimming pools degrades spandex fibers. Figs. 24 and 25 display a 1970s bathing suit that has lost elasticity in its leg bands, which no longer have their original shape. By the late 1990s, garments that had never contained spandex before had small percentages of the elastomer added to improve fit and comfort. Exhibition of garments made with spandex will present serious challenges in the future.

Recommendations for Cleaning, Storing, Handling, and Exhibiting Garments and Accessories with Spandex

- If conservation wet cleaning is essential, use low water temperature and minimize agitation; do not bleach.
- Do not dry clean.
- Do not stretch bands or garments containing spandex while handling, especially if the cracking of brittle filaments can be felt or heard.
- Fold garments with spandex as few times as possible in horizontal

storage and pad folds. Consider horizontal storage for garments with spandex.

- Avoid steam.
- Do not stretch garments with degraded spandex over mannequins; consider other options for display to avoid permanent deformation.
- Monitor fabrics' condition in a prolonged exhibition.

Chronology of Cleaning, Exhibiting, and Storing Problems for Garments and Accessories with Spandex

1962—Light and heat exposure yellowed spandex.[137]

1964—Chlorine bleach harmed spandex.[138]

1970s—Spandex lost its elasticity and permanently deformed over time (Figs. 24 and 25).[139]

1976—Spandex discolored quickly.[140]

1982—High temperatures reduced elasticity.[141]

1982—Dry cleaning caused loss of elasticity in spandex fibers (Fig. 23).[142]

1992—Chlorine compounds yellowed and degraded spandex.[143]

1992—White spandex yellowed with time.[144]

2 Fabric Constructions

Fabric engineers created new fabric constructions throughout the twentieth century. Three of these innovations reportedly caused trouble for cleaners and consumers. A number of companies produced stitch-bonded fabrics for home furnishings and a limited amount of apparel. Engineers also produced pile-weave fake fur and nonwoven imitation suede for cheaper alternatives to fur and leather.

Mali Stitch-Bonded Fabrics

Stitchbonding produces a wide range of fabrics by penetrating and stabilizing a layer of nonwoven fibers, yarns, or film with knitting stitches. The Malimo machine used knit stitches to produce consumer products starting in the 1960s. Variations of the machine also stitched through a web of fibers (Fig. 26). Brand names associated with Mali fabrics are Maliwatt, Arachne, and Araknit (a coating substrate). Malipol pile fabrics imitated natural fur.

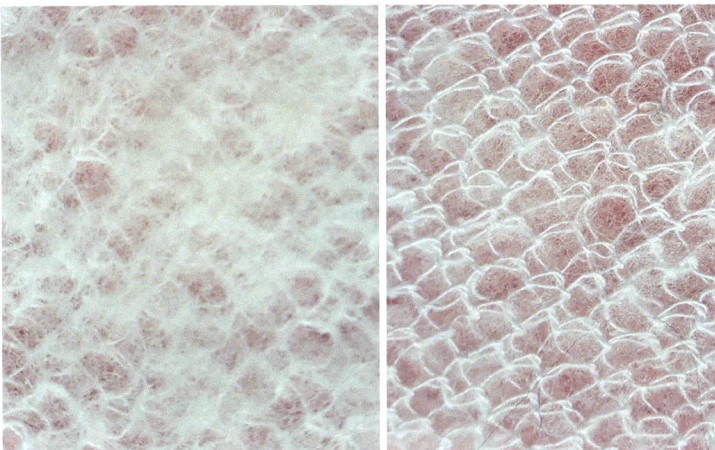

Fig. 26. Mali-type fabric of white cotton warp-knit stitches joining a layer of undyed llama fibers; two views: front (*left*) and (*right*) back on a pink background, circa 1978. Photo taken by Margaret T. Ordoñez. Courtesy of Margaret T. Ordoñez's Sample Textile Collection.

Identification

A common Mali fabric in apparel and drapery has warp and weft yarns held in place by warp-knit stitches. Look for a lack of woven structure and loops of the knit stitches stabilizing the yarns, as in Fig. 27.

Problems with Cleaning and Exhibiting Mali Stitch-Bonded Fabrics

Dry cleaning and professional wet cleaning shrank Mali fabrics. Steaming also shrank and changed the fabrics' dimensions, but these changes could have been fiber related rather than the fault of the structure. Some Mali fabrics contained modacrylic fibers, which would explain heat sensitivity. Problems with Malimo apparel fabrics included fraying and low resilience resulting in bagging at the elbows, knees, and seat.

Recommendations for Cleaning, Storing, Handling, and Exhibiting Mali Stitch-Bonded Fabrics

- Base steaming and conservation wet-cleaning or dry-cleaning decisions on fiber content and soil to be removed.
- Limit the amount of agitation because of the fabric construction.
- Avoid placing folds across the larger set of yarns when storing a Mali fabric in a box; pad fold lines. Roll large, flat pieces of Mali fabric on an acid-free tubes to eliminate folds.
- Avoid snagging yarns when handling an open-construction Mali fabric.
- Consider, when exhibiting them, that Mali fabrics are flexible with good lengthwise stability.

Chronology of Cleaning and Exhibiting Problems for Mali Stitch-Bonded Fabrics

1971—Cleaning and finishing shrank Mali fabrics.[1]
1981—Steaming shrank and dimensionally changed Mali fabrics.[2]

Fake Fur

Fabric engineers created pile fabrics made of various fibers with a woven or knitted base to replicate animal fur by varying the density, length, color, and finish of the pile. Early in the century, they used silk and, particularly, mohair.[3] By mid-century, they made many fake furs of modacrylic, a low-strength heat-sensitive fiber.[4] Fake furs are lighter in weight, more flexible, and more comfortable than

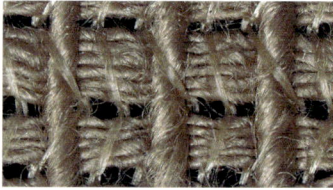

Fig. 27. Malimo stitchbonded casement fabric, circa 1978. Diagonal warp-knit stitches hold warp and weft yarns in place. Photo taken by Margaret T. Ordoñez. Courtesy of Margaret T. Ordoñez's Sample Textile Collection.

real fur. Depending on fiber content, fabric construction, length of pile, and pattern, fake furs had a variety of problems.

Identification

The base of furlike fabrics will be woven or knitted, not the pelt of real fur. If the pile, or "fur," is attached a fabric base, the object is a fake fur (Fig. 28).

Problems with Cleaning, Exhibiting, and Storing Pile-Woven Fake Fur

Cleaning, steaming, and agitating distorted fake furs. Agitation matted, flattened, and removed the fake furs' pile. Professional dry cleaning and wet cleaning disturbed and altered the texture and body. Steaming shrank some fake furs.

Fig. 28. Fake-fur-fabric sample. Photo taken by Margaret T. Ordoñez. Courtesy of Margaret T. Ordoñez's Sample Textile Collection.

Recommendations for Cleaning, Storing, Handling, and Exhibiting Fake Fur

- If conservation wet cleaning is necessary, handwash in warm solution with as little agitation as possible; blot and air dry.
- Avoid commercial dry cleaning because of the heat applied during solvent recovery; spot cleaning or flushing with petroleum solvent (flammable) and air-drying will reduce oily soil.
- Lightly brush the pile if the fibers are in good condition; early natural fibers (silk and mohair) could require more care.
- Hang fake furs in storage with space on either side, to avoid matting and distortion, or lay in a box with as few folds as possible; pad fold lines and avoid placing heavy objects over them.
- Inspect and monitor fake furs that are made of protein fibers for insect infestation.
- Avoid movements that could stress the pile yarns' placement in the woven or knitted structure.
- Do not steam fake furs.
- Support garments made of knitted- or woven-pile fabrics on a mannequin or upper-body form when on display.

Chronology of Cleaning, Exhibiting, and Storing Problems for Fake Fur

1951—Cleaning disturbed and distorted mock-mole-fur fabrics.[5]
1971—Steaming shrank and damaged imitation-fur-pile fabrics.[6]
1973—Agitation during dry cleaning caused loss of design on imitation-fur fabrics (Fig. 29).[7]
1980—Professional wet cleaning and dry cleaning distorted and matted imitation-fur fabrics.[8]

Fig. 29. Imitation fur fabric that lost its pattern during dry cleaning. Courtesy of of Drycleaning and Laundry Institute International (DLI) (*TABS*, 1973).

Fig. 30. Imitation-suede boot, circa 1970s, with permanent creases; two views: boot and close-up. Photo taken by Mark Haran. Courtesy of Iowa State University Textiles and Clothing Museum, 9981828.a.b.

1988—Steaming and professional wet cleaning matted, tufted, and reduced color, texture, and body of imitation-fur-pile fabrics.[9]

1988—Steaming distorted some imitation fur-pile fabrics.[10]

1988—Normal wear distorted and matted imitation-fur-pile fabrics.[11]

1990—Continued wear flattened and distorted imitation-fur-pile fabrics.[12]

Nonwoven Imitation-Suede Fabrics

During the 1930s depression, fabric engineers developed nonwoven imitation suede as a cheaper alternative to true leather suede. Throughout the rest of the century, manufacturers mechanically bonded or hydro-entangled fibers and then brushed or sueded the nonwoven fabric surface to create a suedelike texture.[13] Manufacturers also produced suedelike fabrics with adhesive-attached flock, which is discussed in chapter 5 (67–70).

Identification

If the back of an imitation suedelike fabric is visible, the nonwoven-ground fabric will be obvious. The nonwoven ground also may be visible along creases where the finish has worn, exposing the base. Leather-based suede exhibits some elasticity and is flexible, whereas the nonwoven base would be more rigid.

Problems with Cleaning and Exhibiting Nonwoven-Imitation-Suede Fabrics

Dry cleaning, professional wet cleaning, steaming, and aging damaged nonwoven-imitation-suede fabrics. Over time, the suede dyes faded and discolored; the fabrics stiffened and deformed (Fig. 30). Professional wet cleaning caused some dyes to bleed. Dry cleaning blistered, swelled, discolored, hardened, dissolved, and stiffened some imitation suedes. Moisture from steaming also distorted some imitation suede.

Recommendations for Cleaning, Storing, Handling, and Exhibiting Nonwoven-Imitation-Suede Fabrics

- Considering the frequency of reported problems, do not steam, conservation wet clean, or dry clean nonwoven imitation suede.
- Use a soft brush to clean the surface of nonwoven-imitation-suede fabrics with a vacuum-cleaner nozzle held nearby.
- Fold objects as few times as possible in storage to minimize creases; pad fold lines.
- Avoid creasing these fabrics while handling them.

- Support shoes and other accessories with a fabric-covered batting to maintain the shape in storage and exhibition.
- Support garments made of nonwoven-imitation-suede fabrics on a mannequin or upper-body form when on display.
- Avoid stressing garments of this fabric when adjusting them on a mannequin.

Chronology of Cleaning and Exhibiting Problems for Nonwoven-Imitation-Suede Fabrics

1938—Dry cleaning dissolved imitation-suede leather trimmings.[14]

1938—Steam altered and distorted some imitation-suede trims.[15]

1954—Professional wet cleaning and dry cleaning stiffened and separated imitation-leather trim from the base fabric.[16]

1969—Dry cleaning stiffened some imitation suede (Fig. 31).[17]

1970s—Imitation-suede fabric permanently creased over time (Fig. 30).[18]

1972—Dry cleaning blistered and swelled some imitation-suede coat fabrics, including Heeksuede and Saliksuede brands.[19]

1972—Dry cleaning discolored some all-weather imitation-suede coats.[20]

1980s—Dry cleaning hardened and stiffened imitation suede.[21]

1984—Over time, oxidation caused bright suede colors to fade and become dull.[22]

1988—Some imitation suede dyes were extremely fugitive in water.[23]

1992—Exposure to sunlight and atmospheric gases caused dyes used on artificial suede to fade and change.[24]

Fig. 31. Imitation-suede leather trim sewn to a cardigan wrinkled, stiffened, and became brittle during dry cleaning. Courtesy of DLI (*TABS*, 1969).

3   Printed Components

Printers applied pigments in a thickened paste to fabric surfaces as an inexpensive method to achieve designs. Binders held pigments in place on the fabric surfaces. The printers used several materials as thickeners. Sometimes they used lacquer carriers to form the printing pastes.[1]

Pigment Prints

Pigment printers applied a mixture of insoluble pigments, binders, and a variety of other compounds as a paste to fabric surfaces. Over the century, they used a variety of natural and synthetic materials as binders and thickeners. The printed fabric was heated at a high temperature to cure and fix the resin binder, making it insoluble.[2] The pigment sits on the surface of the fabric, which may be any fiber or color (Figs. 32 and 33). Pigment prints' hand and crock-fastness improved in the later part of the century based on intense research by the printing industry. By the end of the century, more than 80 percent of fabrics marketed in the United States were pigment printed—far surpassing printing with dyes, although a fabric could be printed with both pigments and dyes.[3]

(*Left*) Fig. 32. Pigment-printed design; two views: fabric face and close-up of pigment paste on the fabric. Photo taken by Margaret T. Ordoñez. Courtesy of Margaret T. Ordoñez's Sample Textile Collection.

(*Below*) Fig. 33. Mid-1990s pigment print on a dark ground. Photo taken by Margaret T. Ordoñez. Courtesy of University of Rhode Island Textile Science Collection.

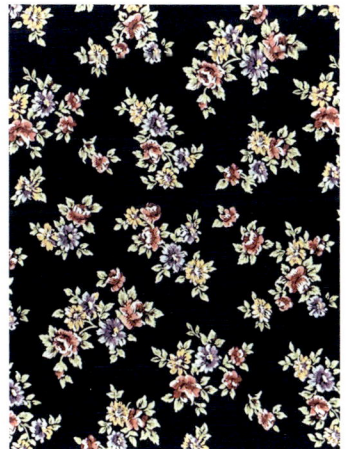

Identification

A pigment covers the surface of the fabric; unlike a dye, it is not absorbed into the fibers. Viewing with a magnifying glass or microscope clearly shows this distinction. In addition, pigments color only the top fabric surface and do not show very distinctly on the back side.

Problems with Cleaning, Exhibiting, and Storing Pigment Prints

Professional wet cleaning, dry cleaning, and aging caused various problems for pigment prints. Dry cleaning stiffened, cracked, curled, and faded the prints. Professional wet cleaning caused similar problems and also loosened the pigments, which could redeposit onto other portions of the garment. Over time, some prints cracked and chipped, leaving a distorted appearance. Abrasion along fold lines resulted in color loss.

Recommendations for Cleaning, Storing, Handling, and Exhibiting Pigment Prints

- Before cleaning, test all prints in water or solvent for solubility. Once a cleaning treatment is chosen based on the soil to be removed, limit agitation to avoid stretching the base fabric underneath the print.
- Do not rub the printed surfaces; pigment prints are sensitive to abrasion.
- If the printed area is stiff or cracked, avoid folding and bending in handling and storage.
- Pad folds when an object's size requires folding in storage.
- Steaming the back side of a pigment print to reduce wrinkles or creases might be more successful than steaming the front side; the steam source should be at least 12 inches from the fabric so that the steam is cool and moist.
- Do not stretch or crease the printed area when dressing a mannequin for exhibition.

Chronology of Cleaning Problems for Pigment Prints

1958—Dry cleaning dissolved a component in some pigment prints.[4]
1958—Dry cleaning dissolved a component in some resin-bonded pigment colors.[5]
1961—Agitation during cleaning removed pigment colors.[6]
1976—Professional wet cleaning softened and removed some pigment prints.[7]

1982—Professional wet cleaning loosened the pigment, which redeposited onto other portions of the garment, causing permanent stains.[8]

1990—Dry cleaning stiffened, cracked, and curled some pigment prints.[9]

1990—Pigment-printed polka dots sometimes cracked and chipped during wear.[10]

1993—Dry cleaning and professional wet cleaning significantly faded pigment prints.[11]

Lacquer Prints

Lacquer printing often is indistinguishable from pigment prints that used a different binder. The roller-printing method for lacquer printing applied insoluble pigments mixed with a lacquer carrier as a printing paste to a fabric. Some lacquer prints contained a plasticizer, which kept them soft and pliable for a period of time.[12] None of the sources from the first half of the century cited in this book mentioned lacquer prints or lacquer finishes. In 1967, *Fairchild's Dictionary of Textiles* listed lacquer finishes that formed "a thin, smooth, highly glazed film on the surface of the cloth; it may be applied in patterns."[13]

Identification

Look for the printing paste that covers the surface of the fabric and does not show much on the back side (Figs. 34 and 35). Laquer-printed designs are more apt to curl than pigment prints.

Fig. 34. Front of sample fabric with white lacquer-dot print on black ground. Courtesy of Drycleaning and Laundry Institute International (DLI) (Lyle, *Focus on Fabrics*, 179).

Problems with Cleaning Lacquer Prints

Lacquer prints cracked, curled, peeled, stiffened, and shriveled during dry cleaning. Solvents dissolved the plasticizers, leaving the fabrics distorted and damaged. The 1980 *Encyclopedia of Textiles* warned that lacquer finishes were "not durable against dry cleaning unless so stated."[14]

Recommendations for Cleaning, Storing, Handling, and Exhibiting Lacquer Prints

- Do not dry clean lacquer-printed garments.
- Conservation wet clean only if essential, since wet cleaning could result in the lacquer separating from the substrate as the fibers swell.
- Be aware of curled edges of lacquer-printed designs; abrasion could cause damage to the prints.
- If the printed area is stiff or cracked, avoid folding and bending in storage.

Fig. 35. Blue and gray lacquer print on dark-blue ground. Courtesy of DLI (Lyle, *Focus on Fabrics*, 115).

- Fold as few times as possible in storage to protect the pigment paste; pad fold lines.
- Steaming the back side of a lacquer print to reduce wrinkles or creases may be more successful than steaming the front side; the steam source should be at least 12 inches from the fabric so that the steam is cool and moist.
- Do not stretch or abrade the printed area when dressing a mannequin for exhibition.

Chronology of Cleaning Problems for Lacquer Prints

1950—Dry cleaning caused lacquer prints to crack, curl, and peel away from the fabric surface.[15]

1958—Dry cleaning dissolved plasticizers in some lacquer prints, leaving a distorted appearance.[16]

1958—Dry cleaning distorted lacquer prints when the solvent dissolved plasticizing oils (Fig. 36).[17]

1974—Dry cleaning dissolved plasticizers in some lacquer prints, stiffening the fabric.[18]

1976—Dry cleaning shriveled and curled some lacquer-stencil prints.[19]

1989—Dry cleaning stiffened lacquer-stencil prints, which curled and peeled from the fabric.[20]

Fig. 36. Dry cleaning removed the plasticizing oils from this lacquer-stencil dot print, causing the circles to shrivel. Courtesy of DLI (Lyle, *Focus on Fabrics*, 442).

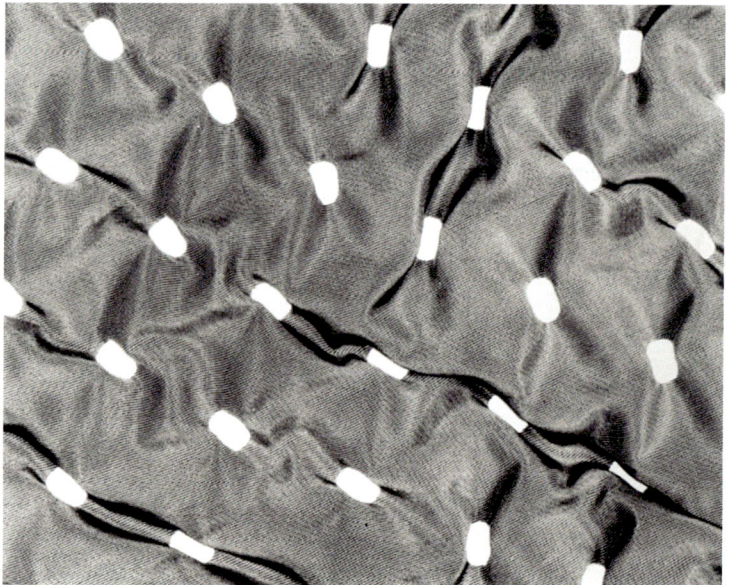

4   Coatings

Coating fabrics on one or both sides with a substance such as lacquer, rubber, or resin created functional and decorative effects. Using coatings, manufacturers produced wind- and water-resistant fabrics, simulated-leather effects, wet looks, and other special effects. Coatings were thick, thin, porous, or nonporous structures. Application of coatings involved dipping a fabric in the solution (fills interstices), spreading the solution with a knife, or calendaring.[1]

Cushion-Cover Fabrics

The coatings on the backside of fabrics stabilized the yarns and secured seams on twentieth-century upholstery fabrics (Fig. 37). Zippers on cushion covers eased manufactures' inserting cushions into the cover but were not intended for consumer usage, which caused misconceptions and problems for the cleaner and consumer. The Federal Trade Commission Care Label Rule did not cover upholstery fabrics; the labeling of these objects was strictly voluntary and often absent, but cleaners still cleaned the covers—sometimes with disastrous results. Shrinkage prevented cushion reinsertion, or fabric color and texture no longer matched corresponding upholstery.[2]

Fig. 37. Coating on the back of a 1973 upholstery fabric to stabilize yarns. Photo taken by Margaret T. Ordoñez. Courtesy of Margaret McWilliams. Swatch 38 in Joseph and Gieseking, *Illustrated Guide to Textiles*.

Identification

Look for an often-heavy coating applied to the back side of upholstery fabrics, especially those with low thread counts and novelty yarns.

Problems with Cleaning and Storing Cushion-Cover Fabrics

Coatings on the fabric's inner surface dissolved during dry cleaning and professional wet cleaning, resulting in a distorted cover. Professional dry cleaning and wet cleaning shrank, raveled, frayed, and reduced the cushion-cover fabric's body. As coatings aged, they stiffened and cracked, and fabric often stretched and lost body.

Recommendations for Cleaning, Storing, Handling, and Exhibiting Cushion-Cover Fabrics

- If a cushion cover exhibits no sign of damage or loss of coating and cleaning is necessary, test the coating in a seam allowance for solubility in water or solvent before cleaning to avoid irreversible damage; minimize heat and agitation.
- If a cushion cover is distorted, conservation wet cleaning and dry cleaning most likely will increase damage.
- Avoid folding coated upholstery fabrics when handling and storing, especially if stiffened.
- Minimize steam; apply cool steam to the top surface if steaming is necessary to reduce wrinkles or creases.
- Provide sufficient support for coated upholstery fabrics on display, especially if the coating has cracked or stiffened.

Chronology of Cleaning Problems for Cushion-Cover Fabrics

1976—Dry cleaning dissolved some cushion-covers' coating and caused fraying, shrinkage, and limpness.[3]

1988—Dry cleaning dissolved some cushion-covers' inner coatings and caused shrinkage, raveling, fraying, and limpness.[4]

1995—Professional wet cleaning and dry cleaning caused some cushion covers to ravel and pull apart.[5]

1995—Dry cleaning dissolved some cushion-covers' adhesives.[6]

Down- and Feather-Filled Garments

Down- and feather-filled coats saturated the outerwear market in the 1980s and 1990s. Down is a fluffy, soft fiber that grows under the outer feathers of ducks, geese, and other waterfowl.[7] Some manufacturers applied coatings on the inner surface of coats' outer fabric to create wind resistance and water repellency and to prevent the down, feathers, and impurities from moving through the fabric. Consumers and cleaners could not determine whether the garment had a durable or nondurable coating before cleaning.[8]

Identification

The construction of down-filled coats, jackets, and vests prevents the underside of the outer fabric from being seen. However, uniform stiffness versus limp fabric in scattered areas, a crackling sound when the fabric is bent, a powdery feel when the fabric is handled, plus the shaft of feathers easily penetrating the fabric are indicators that the condition of a coating has deteriorated.

Problems with Cleaning Down- and Feather-Filled Garments

Reports documented down-coat cleaning problems in the mid-1980s that continued throughout the 1990s. Professional wet cleaning and dry cleaning dissolved many coatings on down-filled coat fabrics. Fig. 38 illustrates down and other impurities showing through the outer fabric after dry-cleaning solvent dissolved the inner coating. In Fig. 39, the oily residue from down feathers stained the coat's outer-fabric surface.

Recommendations for Cleaning, Storing, Handling, and Exhibiting Down- and Feather-Filled Garments

- Vacuum with low suction to avoid pulling feather fragments and impurities to the surface, increasing their visibility.
- If feathers and impurities show through the outer layer of the coat, the coating has dissolved. Conservation wet clean or dry clean with caution because these effects may increase.
- If the garment shows no sign of coating solubilization, test in water or solvent for coating solubility. Be cautious in choosing to conservation wet clean or dry clean; oxidized oils could migrate to the surface, causing discoloration.
- Access and then monitor the condition of coated fabrics in down-filled garments.
- Store garments separately if feathers or impurities are penetrating the fabric surface.
- Avoid storing down-filled garments vertically because feathers tend to settle.

Chronology of Cleaning Problems for Down- and Feather-Filled Coats

1985—Some coatings on down-filled garments dissolved completely, and the feathers penetrated the outer-shell fabric.[9]

1995—Dry cleaning softened and removed some coatings on down-filled garments.[10]

Fig. 38. Down- and feather-filled coat without coating on inner-fabric surface; the coat's coating dissolved during dry cleaning, allowing the dark feathers and impurities to penetrate the outer surface. Courtesy of Drycleaning and Laundry Institute International (DLI) (*Clothes Care Gazette*, January 1997).

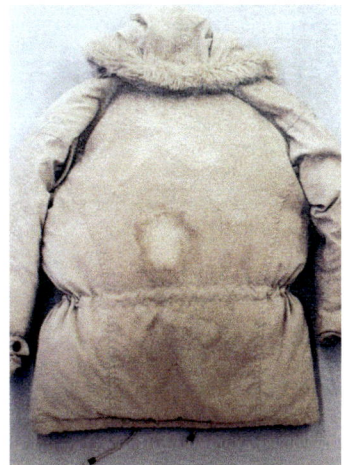

Fig. 39. Down- and feather-filled coat; the oily residue from the down feathers caused discoloration on the outer surface during dry cleaning. Courtesy of DLI (*Clothes Care Gazette*, January 1997).

1996—Professional wet cleaning removed some coatings on down-filled garments.[11]

1997—Dry cleaning solvent dissolved some coatings on down-filled garments and redeposited oily residue on outer fabric (Figs. 38 and 39).[12]

Polyurethane- and Urethane-Coated Fabrics

Based on research in the thirties, urethane and polyurethane resins coated apparel and airplane fabrics during World War II. Commercial production of polyurethane surface coatings, adhesives, and foams began in the 1950s, followed by spandex fibers in the 1960s. Spandex, foams, and foam laminates are discussed in other chapters. Polyurethane- and urethane-coated fabrics offered improved water- and wind-resistance as well as special surface effects such as imitation leather.[13]

Identification

The coating completely covers the base fabric and has a smooth face unless a pattern produces a special effect. It is water resistant or waterproof. Acetone or acetic acid (vinegar) applied on an inconspicuous place like a seam allowance dulls or alters the face of the finish.

Problems with Cleaning Polyurethane- and Urethane-Coated Fabrics

Starting in the early 1970s, publications frequently reported polyurethane- and urethane-coating problems, which continued to the end of the century. Dry cleaning and professional wet cleaning dissolved polyurethane and urethane coatings, which swelled, cracked, blistered, wrinkled, bubbled, and became tacky. Fig. 40 displays a polyurethane-coated jacket that bubbled and blistered after dry cleaning, due to coating solubility; Fig. 41 shows a closeup of the distorted jacket. While drying, the coated fabrics often became tacky, and surfaces stuck together.

Some polyurethane- and urethane-coated fabrics discolored and decomposed over time. Exposure to atmospheric fumes, UV and natural light, and heat accelerated the oxidation and decomposition.[14] As these coatings aged, they became weak and brittle instead of elastic; flexing and stretching caused them to break down completely.[15] Coatings crumbled, bubbled, blistered, became sticky, and separated from the base fabrics during dry cleaning. UV light and aging yellowed clear plastics by inducing chemical changes in the polymer.[16] Liquids also appeared on polyurethane surfaces, resulting from migration of the plasticizer.

Fig. 40. A polyurethane-coated fabric coat. Courtesy of DLI (*Fabric Facts*, December 1971).

Fig. 41. A close-up of the polyurethane-coated coat in Fig. 40. The coating separated from the outer fabric during dry cleaning and caused a bubbled and blistered appearance. Courtesy of DLI (*Fabric Facts*, December 1971).

Recommendations for Cleaning, Storing, Handling, and Exhibiting Polyurethane- and Urethane-Coated Fabrics

- Conservation wet clean only if necessary being aware that the coating could separate from the base fabric; minimize agitation, flexing, and manipulation of a garment when wet cleaning. Do not bleach, heat to dry, or press.
- Wipe surfaces with a damp cloth and detergent solution to remove soil.
- Do not dry clean polyurethane- or urethane-coated fabrics due to the high frequency of reported problems. The probability of further damage is extremely high.
- Identify and isolate polyurethane- and urethane-coated objects in the collection to prevent damage to objects nearby.
- Monitor garments in storage regularly to check for coating decomposition and plasticizer migration; liquid on the surface is an indicator of plasticizer migration.
- Protect from dust.
- Fold as few times as possible in storage; if the surface is sticky, do not wrap objects or pad folds with paper or cotton cloth.
- Prevent coated surfaces from sticking together in storage by separating them with silicone-release paper or shiny fabric made of multi-filament yarns.
- Handle both stable and degraded coated fabrics with caution and only when necessary.
- Steam the back side of the coated fabric, if necessary, to reduce wrinkles or creases; the steam source should be at least 12 inches from the fabric so that the steam is cool and moist.
- Avoid stretching a coated fabric when mounting and adjusting a garment on a mannequin; provide sufficient support for garments on display.
- Minimize light exposure in storage and exhibition, both in time and intensity.
- Provide sufficient air ventilation in storage and display areas to dissipate volatile degradation products.

Chronology of Cleaning, Exhibiting, and Storing Problems for Polyurethane- and Urethane-Coated Fabrics

1971—Dry cleaning bubbled and blistered some polyurethane-coated fabrics (Figs. 40 and 41).[17]

1973—Dry cleaning caused blisters and loss of pattern definition on some urethane-coated imitation leathers.[18]

1975—Dry cleaning caused some polyurethane-coated fabrics to become tacky and stick together.[19]

1977—Dry cleaning dissolved, softened, and wrinkled some poly-urethane-coated fabrics.[20]

1980—Dry cleaning swelled, separated, and blistered some polyure-thane-coated fabrics.[21]

1980—Exposure to light and atmospheric gases partially separated some polyurethane coatings from the base fabric.[22]

1982 –Dry cleaning cracked and separated some urethane-coated fabrics.[23]

1983—Professional wet cleaning discolored, crumbled, disintegrated, and degraded some polyurethane-coated fabrics.[24]

1985—Exposure to light and atmospheric gases caused rapid oxida-tion and deterioration of urethane films.[25]

1987—Polyurethane-coated fabrics discolored slowly over time when exposed to the atmosphere.[26]

1987—Polyurethane-coated fabrics deteriorated and crumbled over time.[27]

1988—Dry cleaning abnormally affected some urethane coatings.[28]

1990—Dry cleaning separated polyurethane coatings from the fabric bases and caused some coated fabrics to self-stick.[29]

1990—Urethane coatings used to make snakeskin trim dissolved dur-ing dry cleaning, which caused bubbling, peeling, and separating from the base fabric.[30]

1994—Some polyurethane coatings self-stuck or separated during dry cleaning.[31]

Polyvinyl Chloride–Coated Fabrics

Based on previous research, in 1926, a B. F. Goodrich scientist look-ing for an alternative to natural rubber plasticized polyvinyl chloride (PVC). Two of the first successful applications of this product were as a water-resistant-fabric coating and molded shoe heels. Plasticizers, added during manufacture, prevented stiffness and made fabrics soft and pliable.[32] Production increased during World War II, and after the war, sales of PVC-coated fabrics never slowed down. Stabilizers and other additives improved PVC goods during the century and helped address health concerns related to the product. Fig. 42 il-lustrates a PVC-coated fabric.

Fig. 42. Back and front of PVC-coated, printed rainwear fabric sample. The back side, on the left, is matte, while the front side, on the right, illustrates the shiny PVC-coated effect. Photo taken by Kelly L. Reddy-Best. Courtesy of University of Rhode Island (URI) Textile Science Collection.

Identification

PVC-coated fabric has a glossy smooth surface on one side unless the fabric has been calendared with a heated roller to imitate a specific material, such as leather. The coating covering the fabric is apparent. The surface of a PVC-resin-coated fabric may feel waxy, and the fabric can have a distinctive smell, like new PVC gloves. If the coating has begun to deteriorate, cracking, stiffening, blooming, weeping, or off-gassing may be apparent.

Problems with Cleaning, Exhibiting, and Storing Polyvinyl Chloride–Coated Fabrics

The Drycleaning and Laundry Institute International bulletins reported an abundance of PVC-coated fabric problems beginning in the mid-1940s and continuing until the end of the century. Dry cleaning and professional wet cleaning caused many problems for PVC-coated fabrics. Agitation during both cleaning procedures caused the coatings to crack and peel. Solvent dissolved many of the early plasticizers used in vinyl, which caused a large number of problems for servicing these fabrics. After the plasticizers began to dissolve in solvent, the fabrics cracked, shrank, bubbled, puckered, and became stiff or shiny. In 1982, DLI reported the availability of high-molecular-weight plasticizers on the market that withstood dry cleaning. Some manufacturers, however, still used the low-molecular-weight plasticizers for various reasons, causing inconsistency for serviceability between brands of garments.

PVC coatings degraded chemically and physically over time. Besides cracking of the coating, the most obvious signs of chemical degradation included yellowing and darkening. High temperatures and light induced the release of hydrochloric acid as the plastic degraded, which caused the PVC coating and base fabric to fade or change color. Degrading PVC released acidic vapors strong enough to attack adjacent fabrics. Migration of stabilizers and plasticizers also resulted in blooming, weeping, discoloring, and losing flexibility. [33] The three PVC-coated fabrics in Fig. 43 are good examples of how coating degrades over time. Their surfaces felt sticky where they overlapped, and the silver coating discolored the lower gold fabric in Fig. 44 and has stuck to the upper green fabric, shown in Fig. 45.

Although some PVC coatings appeared stable, other subtle signs indicated decomposition. Gradual release of acids often caused metal components to corrode, a sign that degradation has begun. Also, a sharp, acidic smell indicates decomposition. [34]

Recommendations for Cleaning, Storing, Handling, and Exhibiting Polyvinyl Chloride–Coated Fabrics

- Practice extreme caution when cleaning vinyl-coated fabrics. Damage is irreversible and permanent once the plasticizer is lost. Considering the frequency of reported problems from 1940 to the end of the century, cleaning decisions must be made carefully. If the coating is not cracked, clean the surface with deionized water or a low-concentration surfactant solution applied with a slightly

Fig. 43. Three PVC-coated mid-1990s fabric samples (green, silver, and gold) folded in the center, overlapped, and stapled to a sample card. Photo taken by Kelly L. Reddy-Best. Courtesy of URI Textile Science Collection.

Fig. 44. Degraded PVC coatings resulted in the mid-1990s silver and gold fabrics sticking to each other, causing dark discoloration on the gold fabric. Photo taken by Kelly L. Reddy-Best. Courtesy of URI Textile Science Collection.

Fig. 45. Silver PVC-coated mid-1990s fabric sample stuck to the green PVC-coated mid-1990s fabric and discolored the green surface. Photo taken by Kelly L. Reddy-Best. Courtesy of URI Textile Science Collection.

dampened swab. If coating is not intact, avoid wetting. Avoid solvents, including dry-cleaning solvents, that could dissolve plasticizers.[35]

- Degradation is inevitable and irreversible. Promptly isolate PVC-coated objects, storing them separately from all other objects.
- Handle PVC-coated garments with caution and only when necessary; consider wearing nitrile gloves when handling these objects.
- Protect from dust.
- Prevent coated surfaces from sticking together in storage by separating them with silicone-release paper rather than tissue or cloth.
- Do not store in polyethylene bags or boxes; the plasticizer in the PVC degrades polyethylene. Slow degradation by enclosing PVC objects in nonabsorbent media such as glass, polypropylene boxes, or a container made of polyester film (Mylar and Melinex).[36]
- Do not place in low-temperature storage; PVC becomes brittle in the cold.[37]
- Do not iron or press PVC-coated fabrics; limit steaming, and if steaming is necessary, apply steam to the back of the fabric and avoid hot steam—hold steam source at least 12 inches away from the object to provide cool moisture.
- Avoid stressing coated fabrics when arranging a garment on a mannequin. Provide support to garments and accessories made of PVC-coated fabrics.
- Exhibit degrading PVC-coated objects in an isolated space because their off-gassing creates an unhealthy microenvironment for adjacent objects.

Chronology of Cleaning, Exhibiting, and Storing Problems for Polyvinyl Chloride–Coated Fabrics

1946—Dry cleaning dissolved some plasticizers used in vinyl coatings, leaving garment distorted.[38]

1946—Dry cleaning stiffened, cracked, and broke some vinyl-coated fabrics.[39]

1946—Agitation during professional wet cleaning caused vinyl-coated fabrics to crack and peel.[40]

1946—Matte vinyl-coated fabrics became shiny after professional wet cleaning and dry cleaning.[41]

1947—Dry cleaning dissolved plasticizers in vinyl coatings on rayon coats, leaving the garments stiff and cracked.[42]

1963—Vinyl-coated draperies became stiff and bubbled on the surface during dry cleaning.[43]

1973—Dry cleaning dissolved some vinyl trims' plasticizers, decreasing softness and flexibility.[44]

1973—Dry cleaning caused loss of low-molecular-weight plasticizers, which resulted in loss of softness and flexibility.[45]

1973—Dry cleaning shrank some vinyl coatings.[46]

1976—Some vinyl coatings stiffened and cracked over time.[47]

1980s—A circa 1980s Claude Montana PVC-coated black patent-leather jacket was accessioned in "good condition" in 2000. In a 2006 collection survey, the left lapel had adhered to the left front, and the surface felt "sticky."[48]

1982—Manufacturers marketed high-molecular-weight plasticizers that withstood dry cleaning.[49]

1988—Dry cleaning stiffened and cracked some vinyl.[50]

1989—Dry cleaning dissolved plasticizers in the vinyl-coated backings of belts, resulting in stiffening, shrinking, and puckering.[51]

Mid-1990s—Degraded PVC coatings stuck to and discolored adjacent fabrics (Figs. 43, 44, and 45).[52]

1996—Big Ben jelly-style blue sandals designed by Patricia Cox had begun to lose their shape and become rigid when examined in 2006; the PVC uppers' surface was "extremely sticky."[53]

Rubber-Coated Fabrics

Extensive research on coating fabrics with rubber begun in the nineteenth century continued into the twentieth, with waterproof rainwear being one of the end products. Apparel collections may include early garments that have rubber-coated dress shields. In the twenties, rubber coatings waterproofed silk and cotton fabrics. Rubber-coated cotton fabrics functioned as hospital sheeting (one or both sides coated), crib sheets, and infants' pants.[54] Reports described rubber coatings causing frequent cleaning problems for the fabrics from the 1950s to the end of the century. However, collections with rubber-coated fabrics also have to deal with the problems associated with cured rubber aging, resulting in the coating hardening, becoming brittle, and cracking.

Identification

A rubber coating will completely cover one or both sides of the fabric. The problems listed above related to aging may be apparent; they help identify rubber coatings. A distinctive rubber odor might be present. Because of toxic fumes, burn tests are not advisable.

Problems with Cleaning, Exhibiting, and Storing Rubber-Coated Fabrics

From the start of the century, rubber coatings presented problems even when new. They emitted an odor, stiffened, and degraded during use.[55] Dry cleaning stiffened, separated, blistered, bubbled, and caused stickiness on rubber-coated rainwear. The problems sometimes occurred after one dry cleaning or professional wet cleaning and often

Fig. 46. Rubber-coated fabric. The coating on the fabric blistered and bubbled during dry cleaning. Courtesy of DLI (*Fabrics and Fashions*, March 1994).

became progressively worse after each treatment. The adhesives dissolved in solvent, causing varying degrees of fabric distortion, as in Fig. 46, which shows a blistered and bubbled rubber-coated fabric after dry cleaning. Fig. 47 displays a 1950s rubber-coated car coat; the coating separated from the outer fabric during dry cleaning. Particular coated-rainwear brands that experienced significant cleaning difficulties during the late 1950s included Snowdrift, K. L. T. Product, Mallo, Comfort, Jingle Bells, and Strength.[56]

Rubber-coated rainwear cracked, yellowed, and degraded over time, causing fabrics to self-stick and produce a chemical smell. Stiffening also is an inherent problem. Some rubber-coated raincoats from the 1970s through the end of the century instantly puckered and distorted when steamed.

Fig. 47. The rubber coating on a 1950s car coat separated from the outer fabric during dry cleaning. Courtesy of DLI (*Fabric Facts*, August 1959).

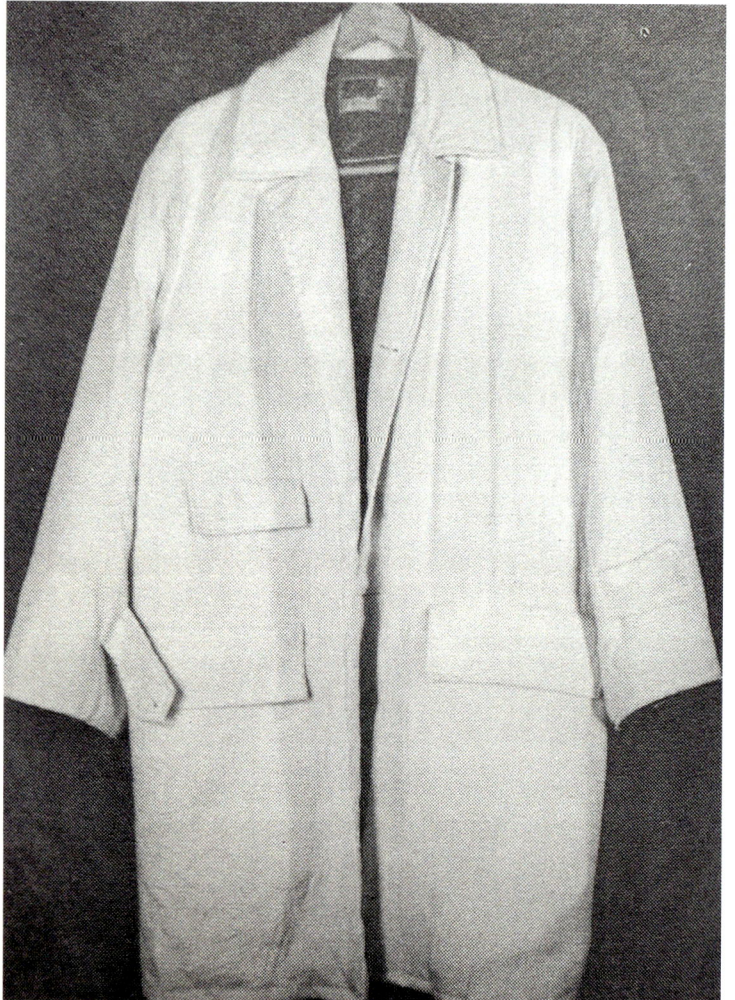

Recommendations for Cleaning, Storing, Handling, and Exhibiting Rubber-Coated Fabrics

- If surface is not sticky, limit cleaning to low-suction vacuuming and wiping it with slightly damp microfiber cloth. If surface is sticky, isolate object and consider deaccessioning.
- Identify and isolate rubber-coated rainwear. Routinely monitor garments in storage every six months and on exhibition for off-gassing; consider deaccessioning if isolation is not possible.
- Check women's dresses for degraded dress shields that could be made with rubber-coated fabrics; photograph and document them in situ before removing them. (Dress shields made from a variety of materials throughout the century often have degraded from unstable compounds as well as aged perspiration.)
- Store in a cool, dark, dry, oxygen-free environment to slow rubber degradation. Protect from dust.
- Avoid folding aging rubber-coated fabrics in flat storage, pad folds, and separate layers with silicone-release paper to avoid self-sticking.
- Handle with caution because stiffened coatings are brittle.
- Do not steam or press with an iron.
- Avoid stretching rubber-coated garments when adjusting them on a mannequin; provide sufficient support for garments and accessories in an exhibit.
- Monitor fabrics' condition in a prolonged exhibition.

Chronology of Cleaning, Exhibiting, and Storing Problems for Rubber-Coated Fabrics

1900–onward—Rubber-coated fabrics emitted an odor, degraded, and stiffened during use.

1958—Dry cleaning stiffened some rubber-coated rainwear fabrics.[57]

1958—Some rubber-coated rainwear fabrics cracked and yellowed over time.[58]

1959—Rubber coatings on car coats separated from the outer fabric during dry cleaning (Fig. 47).[59]

1970s—Rubber-coated raincoats had a 50 percent chance of stability loss if steamed.[60]

1970s—Rubber coatings on raincoats broke down over time, causing fabrics to stick together and have a chemical smell.[61]

1978—Dry cleaning caused the rubber coating to separate and blister.[62]

1978—Dry cleaning blistered the surface of some rubber-coated fabrics.[63]

1980s—Coated raincoats had a 50 percent chance of stability loss if steamed.[64]

1987—Some rubber-coated raincoats bubbled and blistered after one dry cleaning.[65]

1989—Certain rubber finishes did not withstand dry cleaning.[66]

1994—Some rubber-coated raincoats self-stuck and separated during dry cleaning.[67]

1994—Rubber-coated fabrics blistered and bubbled during dry cleaning (Fig. 46).[68]

1994—Some rubber-coated raincoats puckered after steaming.[69]

5 Adhesives

Adhesives bonded many twentieth-century fabrics, ornaments, and structural supports. They adhered buttons, beads, sequins, glitter, rhinestones, cork, and felt to base fabrics, instead of stitching. Manufacturers bonded fabrics, interlinings, seams, interfacings, and flocked designs to add support, decrease production time and costs, or create a desired appearance.

Garments and Accessories with Bonded Ornamentation

Problems with adhesive-adhered trims to garments began as early as the 1930s. Funfelt garments, popular in the 1960s (shown in Figs. 48 and 49), had large bonded-felt cutouts in a variety of patterns

(*Left*) Fig. 48. Six 1960s Funfelt garments. Courtesy of Drycleaning and Laundry Institute International (DLI) (*Fabric Facts*, February 1968).

(*Below*) Fig. 49. Felt cut-outs on the dress on the left in Fig. 48. The cut-outs curled and distorted because perchlorethylene softened the bonding adhesive. Courtesy of DLI (*Fabric Facts*, February 1968).

and shapes adhered to the fashions. These garments probably were designs for the home-sewing market, and in 1969, Dritz offered Stitch Witchery to that market. This thin sheet of polyamide strands fused layers of fabric together when thermally activated with an iron. Pellon's Wonder-Under, also a polyamide-based fusible web, became available commercially in 1986. HeatnBond, available in 1989, was a polyvinyl alcohol "iron-on adhesive," known to stiffen over time. Research on these three products offers results that inform collection caretakers of homesewn garments, although the products also could have been used in garments and accessories for the retail market. Until the end of the century, manufacturers and home sewers adhered ornaments to various types of garments, sometimes without considering their serviceability.

Identification

Ornamentations are not affixed to a base fabric with stitches, which would be a traditional method of attachment. The adhesive might be visible at the point of contact, especially if it has yellowed with age. Aging might have weakened an adhesive's hold so that the ornamentation is loosened.

Problems with Cleaning, Exhibiting, and Storing Garments and Accessories with Bonded Ornamentation

In 1940, the National Association of Dyers and Cleaners (NADC) Bulletin Service provided its first documentation of an adhered-ornament care problem; subsequent publications frequently reported similar issues. Ornament adhesives caused many problems in dry cleaning. They often dissolved in dry-cleaning solvents or water, resulting in partial or complete loss of the ornamentation. The decorative pieces also distorted, curled, or peeled during cleaning, leaving the garment or object with an undesirable appearance because heat or solvent affected the adhesive.

A 1987 Clothes Care Gazette bulletin reported the adhesives that glued rhinestones to a fabric were not resistant to dry-cleaning solvent, and after one cycle, the rhinestones fell off. Various reports indicate problems occurred after either one or several dry cleanings. Additionally, agitation during commercial wet cleaning also removed some ornaments.

Adhesives also failed over time. Fig. 50 displays garments with large and small adhesive-bonded rhinestones. Fig. 51 shows close-ups of designs where the rhinestones completely or partially detached.

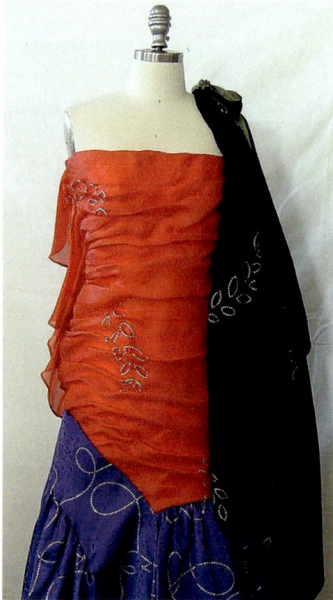

Fig. 50. Dress with small glued-on rhinestones from the spring 1984 Arnold Scaasi line; style number 8558. Photo taken by Kelly L. Reddy-Best. Courtesy of University of Rhode Island Historic Textile and Costume Collection (URI HTCC), 1997.01.24, Donor: Arnold Scaasi Studio, NYC.

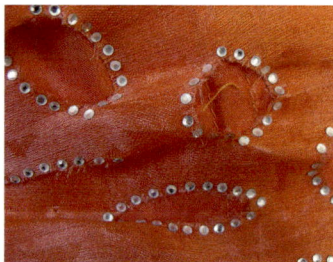

Fig. 51. Small adhered rhinestones encircling cut-outs; some partially or completely detached from the base fabric in Fig. 50. Photo taken by Kelly L. Reddy-Best. Courtesy of URI HTCC, 1997.01.24, Donor: Arnold Scaasi Studio, NYC.

Recommendations for Cleaning, Storing, Handling, and Exhibiting Garments and Accessories with Bonded Ornamentation

- Check that glued-on ornaments are firmly attached before vacuuming with low suction or cleaning. Test all ornament adhesives in an inconspicuous area for solvent or water solubility before cleaning. Also, be aware of agitation levels because even light agitation could partially or completely remove ornamentation.
- Avoid folding an area with a concentration of glued-on ornaments, such as the neckline of a dress.
- Use a dust cover over a garment in hanging storage to protect glued-on ornaments and avoid damage to adjacent garments.
- When handling, check for loose ornaments and dry, peeling adhesive that does not provide a firm hold on ornaments so that they will not fall off or be lost. Loosened trim or ornamentation could catch on itself or fabric surfaces when an object is moved or another object comes into contact with its surface.
- Steam fabrics or garments that have ornamentation glued on carefully; the heat and moisture could soften adhesives.
- Be aware when placing garments on supports for exhibition that glued-on ornaments might not be securely held on; avoid stressing areas with glued-on ornaments when dressing a mannequin.

Chronology of Cleaning Problems for Garments and Accessories with Bonded Ornamentation

1939—Velvet trim bonded to a satin material separated completed during dry cleaning and partially separated during commercial wet cleaning.[1]

1940—Sequin adhesive dissolved in dry-cleaning solvent.[2]

1951—Glitter removed after one dry cleaning.[3]

1968—Felt cutout adhesive dissolved during dry cleaning (Figs. 48 and 49).[4]

1984—Adhered rhinestones partially or completely detached from the base fabric over time (Figs. 50 and 51).[5]

1985—Slight agitation removed glitter during commercial wet cleaning.[6]

1986—Pellon's Wonder-Under, marketed this year, exhibited significant product bleed-through, producing an unacceptable appearance and significant stiffening in accelerated-aging tests.[7]

1987—Rhinestone adhesive dissolved in dry-cleaning solvent.[8]

1988—Cork-trim adhesive dissolved in dry-cleaning solvent.[9]

1988—Leather- and suede-trim adhesive softened and dissolved in dry-cleaning solvent.[10]

1989—HeatnBond, available this year, exhibited undesirable yellowing, bleed-through, and loss of bonding strength in accelerated-aging tests.[11]

1990—Adhesive softened causing glitter removal after one dry cleaning.[12]

1993—Button adhesive dissolved in dry-cleaning solvent.[13]

1995—Trim and bead adhesive not resistant to dry cleaning.[14]

1996—Glitter adhesive dissolved during dry cleaning with partial or complete loss.[15]

Bonded and Laminated Fabrics

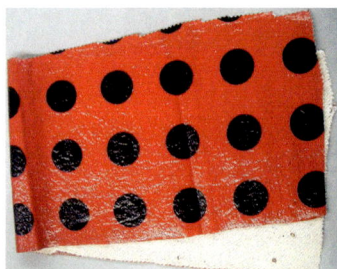

Fig. 52. Front and back of a delaminated fabric; an adhesive bonded the heavy red and black film to a white knit backing fabric. Photo taken by Kelly L. Reddy-Best. Courtesy of URI Textile Science Collection.

Beginning mid-century, converters used adhesives to join fabric to fabric, fabric to film, fabric to foam, or fabric to foam to fabric. Sources inconsistently applied the terms *bonded* and *laminated* to these multilayer fabrics. Adhesives joined a face fabric or film to a lining such as tricot and jersey knits, which were flexible and inexpensive, to add stability and body or provide warmth. Polyurethane foam, joined with an adhesive to a face fabric, also could be adhered to a lining fabric, creating a three-layer structure. The lamination technique also joined fabrics and films, such as polyvinyl chloride sheets or Gore-Tex, which transmitted moisture; Figs. 52 and 53 illustrate fabrics adhered to a film.[16] Manufacturers originally applied adhesives in thin layers, and in the 1970s they introduced small-dot application patterns.

Fig. 53. Front and back of a delaminated fabric; an adhesive bonded the white knit backing fabric to the brown film with an imitation leather, heat-embossed pattern. Photo taken by Kelly L. Reddy-Best. Courtesy of URI Textile Science Collection.

Identification

A multilayer fabric structure is one identifying characteristic of bonded and laminated fabrics. If the adhesive has begun to fail and layers have begun to separate, identification is even easier. Stiffening of the multilayer fabric also is possible. Note that if foam had been part of the layering, it probably has begun to disintegrate, if not become totally powdered.

Problems with Cleaning, Exhibiting, and Storing Bonded and Laminated Fabrics

The documented problems with bonded and laminated fabrics began in the 1960s and continued to the end of the century. Specific bonded-fabric combinations experienced problems during various periods throughout the century. An example is the separation of acetate and wool fabrics bonded to tricot knits during 1967. Fabric-foam-fabric composites failed repeatedly during cleaning in the 1960s, 1970s, and 1990s. In 1966, nylon fabrics with foam-laminate backings peeled away after one dry cleaning. In the 1970s and 1990s, bonded skiwear fabrics had serious separation problems.

Another major problem occurred when the backing and face fabrics separated after they shrank unevenly during cleaning. Dry cleaning dissolved the adhesive, causing shrinkage and separation of the two layers. The shrinkage resulted in a rippled, blistered, bubbled, and puckered appearance; some fabrics grew significantly stiffer after cleaning and over time. Fig. 54 displays a bonded fabric whose adhesives on the lining yellowed and stiffened over time. Sometimes, full separation occurred after only one dry-cleaning cycle. Fig. 55 illustrates a garment that developed a blistered appearance from the separation of the outer silk layer and foam lining. Agitation during both commercial wet cleaning and dry cleaning also contributed to separation. Adhesives failed in fabric samples that had never undergone any cleaning treatment.

Fig. 54. A yellow and white gingham bonded to a wider white backing fabric that stiffened and discolored over time; note the yellowed remnants of the adhesive on the backing fabric. The bond attaching the two fabrics also failed, and the gingham easily pulled away from the backing. Photo taken by Kelly L. Reddy-Best. Courtesy of URI Textile Science Collection.

Recommendations for Cleaning, Storing, Handling, and Exhibiting Bonded and Laminated Fabrics

- Limit cleaning of bonded objects with obvious delamination or shrinkage to low-suction vacuuming because the adhesive is failing or the two fabrics reacted differently in previous cleaning.
- To remove dust on the surface of a bonded fabric, use a soft brush to lightly brush dust into a vacuum wand held nearby. Strong suction might pull powdered foam to the surface. See section on foams in chapter 7 (97–100).
- Exercise extreme caution if a bonded fabric (no foam) with no evident adhesive failure must be cleaned. Adhesives will have aged and might not retain a secure bond. Test the fabric in an unobtrusive area for delamination and shrinkage before submersing it in water or dry-cleaning solvent. Closely monitor agitation levels during conservation wet cleaning and dry cleaning to avoid separation. Do not use either of these cleaning methods if foam is present.
- Handle, move, and bend fabrics laminated with foam, which most likely has decomposed, with extreme caution.
- If storing in a box, fold garments made of bonded fabric as few times as possible and pad fold lines to avoid stress at the fabric-adhesive interface.
- Consider that aged adhesives might no longer have a strong bond. Slight stress can cause failure of the adhesive holding the layers together. Separation can occur during handling, folding for storage, steaming, dressing a mannequin, or stretching one or both of the layers in bonded or laminated fabrics.

Fig. 55. A 1968 coat with an outer silk fabric bonded to a polyurethane-foam lining that blistered the surface of the fabric during dry cleaning. Courtesy of DLI (*TABS*, 1968).

Chronology of Cleaning Problems for Bonded and Laminated Fabrics

1966—Bonded nylon and foam separated during dry cleaning and resulted in increased stiffness.[17]

1967—Acetate bonded with a tricot-knit separated during dry cleaning.[18]

1967—Wool and acetate fabrics bonded with a tricot lining separated during dry cleaning.[19]

1968—The surface of fabrics bonded to a polyurethane-foam lining blistered on the surface of the fabric during dry cleaning (Fig. 55).[20]

1970s—Adhesives used to bond foam-laminated skiwear garments often failed, causing separation.[21]

1970s—Many adhesives in bonded fabrics failed during commercial wet cleaning and dry cleaning.[22]

1980—Urethane foams bonded to an outer fabric separated during dry cleaning due to solubilization of the adhesive.[23]

1978—Complete separation of bonded fabrics occurred after one dry cleaning.[24]

1985—Bonded fabric separated during cleaning causing a rippling effect.[25]

1991—Gore-Tex components shrank during commercial wet cleaning, causing puckering and differential shrinkage.[26]

1991—Bonded fabrics separated during cleaning, causing a rippling and bubbling effect.[27]

1992—Bonded fabrics separated during cleaning, causing blistering and puckering.[28]

1993—Bonded-foam fabrics resulted in separation and a bubbled appearance from dry cleaning and commercial wet cleaning.[29]

Fusible Interfacings and Interlinings

Fig. 56. Interlining inside front panels of a 1990s Pendleton jacket. Photo taken by Margaret T. Ordoñez. Courtesy of Margaret T. Ordoñez's closet.

Although garments did not typically have interfacings and interlinings at the beginning of the century, by mid-century manufacturers and home sewers inserted woven interfacings and interlinings in garments to give the fabric shape, stability, and stiffness (Fig. 56). Nonwoven interfacings became popular in the fifties, followed by fusible interfacings and interlinings in the sixties. Manufacturers coated interfacings with a layer of adhesive and fused them to a facing with heat and pressure on the cuffs and collars of dress shirts as well as collars, necklines and lapels, pocket flaps, waistbands, and fronts of suits and jackets. The fused facing and interfacing eliminated the need for basting or temporary stitching in clothing construction.[30]

Manufacturers inserted interlinings between two fabrics for additional warmth often in winter coats and quilts. Fusible interlining fabrics ranged from heavy batting to lighter fleece or flannel materials.[31] Nonwoven interlining fabrics began to be used in the eighties.[32]

Identification

Interfacings and interlining may not be visible on garments, but if necklines and other areas are stiffer than the body of a garment, the inner supports probably are present. If adhesives have failed, the facing and face fabric can be separated; remnants of the adhesives may remain.

Problems with Cleaning and Exhibiting Fusible Interfacings and Interlinings

During cleaning procedures, fusible interfacings and interlinings sometimes separated from the fabric to which they were adhered. Differential shrinkage during commercial wet cleaning, dry cleaning, and steaming caused shrinkage and separation of the interfacing and outer fabric creating bubbling, rippling, partial or complete separation, puckering, and permanent wrinkling. One report indicated dry cleaning disintegrated the wool and nonwoven layer of a quilted interlining bonded with neoprene—a synthetic rubber introduced in the thirties.

Staining occurred during cleaning of fabrics with fusible interfacings. During cleaning, some adhesives dissolved and seeped through to the outer fabric, staining the surface. Fig. 57 illustrates a collar coated with excessive adhesive; when the shirt was pressed, the adhesive softened, spread, and penetrated the top layer of the shirting fabric, giving a grey appearance. Stains appeared on the outer surface of the jacket in Fig. 58 after cleaning. Fig. 59 displays a jacket that shows stains in the interfaced area from the adhesive migrating during dry cleaning. Manufacturers and home sewers sometimes adhered fusible interfacings to the back of the face fabric rather than a facing or lining, making separation, staining, and stiffening more apparent.

Recommendations for Cleaning, Storing, Handling, and Exhibiting Fusible Interfacings and Interlinings

- Vacuum with low suction to remove surface particulates, but move and handle carefully while vacuuming.
- Even if a garment with fusible interfacings and interlinings displays no obvious loss of adhesion, consider that adhesives often do not age well. Be cautious in choosing to conservation wet clean or dry clean.
- Be aware that if a garment exhibits separation or shrinkage, conservation wet cleaning or dry cleaning most likely will increase the problem. Removal of adhesive stains is highly unlikely without creating further discoloration.

Fig. 57. A collar adhered to an interfacing coated with excessive adhesive. When the shirt was pressed, the adhesive softened, spread, and penetrated the top layer of the shirting fabric, giving a gray and mottled appearance. Courtesy of DLI (*LABS*, 1977).

Fig. 58. An interfaced jacket with the adhesive applied to the fabric in small dots that appeared on the surface after drying in a warm tumbler because the manufacturer used a heat-sensitive adhesive that melted and stained the outer fabric. Courtesy of DLI (*TABS*, 1968).

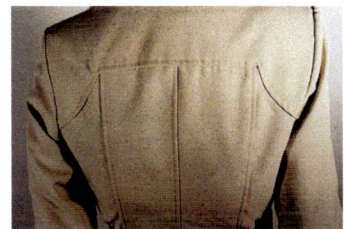

Fig. 59. A jacket with a fusible interfacing. The adhesive on the jacket's fusible material softened when exposed to solvent or the heat of pressing, which caused dark stains on the left shoulder and waistline. Courtesy of DLI (*TABS*, 1985).

- For horizontal storage, use as large a box as possible to minimize the number of folds in a garment with a fused interlining; pad fold lines to avoid stress.
- Handle with minimal bending of garments and accessories to avoid stressing a fused area where the adhesive is failing or has stiffened.
- Be aware that pressing or steaming a garment with a fusible interlining could result in changes in the fabric's surface due to the migration of the adhesive; since pressing is a questionable treatment, test results in an inconspicuous place such as a seam allowance. If steaming is necessary, the source of the steam needs to be at least 12 inches from the fabric so that the steam is cool and wet.
- Avoid stressing garments with fused underfacings as they are positioned and adjusted on mannequins; provide proper support to garments, especially for a lengthy exhibition time.

Chronology of Cleaning and Exhibiting Problems for Fusible Interfacings and Interlinings

1962—White wool and nonwoven sheets, part of a quilted interlining bonded with neoprene, disintegrated during dry cleaning due to adhesive failure.[33]

1968—Adhesive applied in dots on an interfaced jacket appeared on the surface after drying in a warm tumbler (Fig. 58).[34]

1970s—Fusible interfacings on cuffs and collars of men's white dress shirts and suits bubbled when pressed.[35]

1973—Some men's coats' outer fabric separated from the fusible interlining fabric after dry cleaning.[36]

1977—When continuously pressed, the top layer of collars coated with too much adhesive discolored (Fig. 57).[37]

1988—Some fusible interfacings separated from the outer-shell fabric during commercial wet cleaning.[38]

1983—Some men's shirts with fusible interfacing fabrics puckered and permanently wrinkled after laundering.[39]

1983—Some collars and cuffs formed a grey and shiny outline of the fusible interfacing on the outer fabric when steamed.[40]

1985—The adhesive on the fusible material of a jacket softened when exposed to solvent or the heat of pressing and caused dark stains on the face fabric (Fig. 59).[41]

1988—Some fusible interfacings on garments bubbled, blistered, or completely separated from the outer fabric during cleaning.[42]

1991—Some fusible-interfacing adhesives stained the outer garments on collars, cuffs, front plackets, and pocket flaps during dry cleaning.[43]

1991—Some interfacings shrank more than the outer fabric, causing a puckered appearance.[44]

1993—Fabrics with fusible interfacings blistered or rippled during dry cleaning.[45]

1994—Some interfacings lacked resistance to cleaning.[46]

1995—Some fusible interfacings partially or completely separated from the fabric during dry cleaning.[47]

1995—Some interfacings used heat-sensitive adhesives, which seeped through to the surface fabric, forming dark stains when exposed to heat.[48]

1995—Some adhesive or bonding agents used to attach fusible-interfacing material softened and dissolved during dry cleaning.[49]

1995—Some adhesives used on fusible interfacings softened, leached through, and stained the shell fabric when steamed.[50]

1998—Some collars and cuffs of shirts distorted or bubbled because the fused interfacing shrank and separated during commercial wet cleaning.[51]

Chem Stitch Fabrics

Marketed in 1963, Chem Stitch was a chemical-laminating process that bonded two fabrics or fabric and foam with an adhesive in a variety of patterns to create a deeply indented or three-dimensional look simulating stitched quilting. The adhesive technique created artificial-quilted patterns on jackets, blankets, and linings, replacing traditional stitching techniques with a faster adhesive-based construction method.[52] This laminating process soon was replaced by ultrasonic welding, also called ultrasonic sewing or quilting, of thermoplastic fabrics. This method also had durability problems but does not pose a threat to collection holdings.

Identification

The three-dimensional effect in the multilayer fabric is achieved without stitches or woven double-cloth construction. The adhesive likely will have darkened and may be visible.

Problems with Cleaning and Storage of Chem Stitch Fabrics

Chem Stitch adhesives often failed during cleaning. The fabric separated from the foam or fabric backing during commercial wet cleaning and dry cleaning. Figs. 60 and 61 illustrate the resulting bubbled and blistered appearance. Adhesives also discolored over time, as shown in Figs. 62 and 63.

Fig. 60. A 1968 chemically quilted rayon-pile velvet evening coat that partially separated from its lining during its first dry cleaning. Courtesy of DLI (*Fabric Facts*, April 1968).

(*Right*) Fig. 61. A 1968 chemically quilted cotton-pile velvet coat that partially separated from the backing material after multiple dry cleanings. Courtesy of DLI (*Fabric Facts*, April 1968).

Fig. 62. A 1973 three-dimensional Chem Stitch swatch with diagonal lines of adhesive that yellowed over time. Photo taken by Margaret T. Ordoñez. Courtesy of Margaret McWilliams. Swatch 50 in Joseph and Gieseking, *Illustrated Guide to Textiles*.

Fig. 63. The circa 1978 Chem Stitch sample in Fig. 62 with discolored adhesive lines viewed from the back. Photo taken by Margaret T. Ordoñez. Courtesy of Margaret McWilliams. Swatch 50 in Joseph and Gieseking, *Illustrated Guide to Textiles*.

Recommendations for Cleaning, Storing, Handling, and Exhibiting Chem Stitch Fabrics

- Considering failures in the 1960s, limit cleaning to low-suction vacuuming because removal of the discoloration is not possible. Do not pull a vacuum tool across the surface of the fabric, stressing the points of adhesion.
- For horizontal storage, use as large a box as possible to minimize the number of folds; pad fold lines to avoid stress.
- Avoid stressing the adhesive-joined layers to prevent their separating.
- In preparation for exhibition, use a minimum of cool steam on Chem Stitch garments; steam inconspicuous areas first to test the result. Minimize the amount of steam and hold the steam nozzle at least 12 inches from the garment so the steam is cool and wet.

- Avoid stressing garments made by the Chem Stitch techniques as they are positioned and adjusted on mannequins.

Chronology of Cleaning and Exhibiting Problems for Chem Stitch Fabrics

1965—Chem Stitch adhesive dissolved during commercial wet cleaning and dry cleaning.[53]

1968—Chem Stitch adhesive dissolved during dry cleaning (Figs. 60 and 61).[54]

1978—Chem Stitch adhesive discolored over time (Figs. 62 and 63).[55]

Flocked Fabrics

Flocking is a surface effect imitating a pile or nap (Figs. 64, 65, and 66). In the nineteenth century, wallpaper manufacturers created a suedelike pattern on paper by adhering very short fibers (flocks) to the surface with an adhesive; the fibers generally laid parallel to the surface of the paper. In the 1930s, fabric producers began using an electrostatic procedure that aligned the flocks perpendicular to the adhesive-covered cloth. A 1945 text described the process:

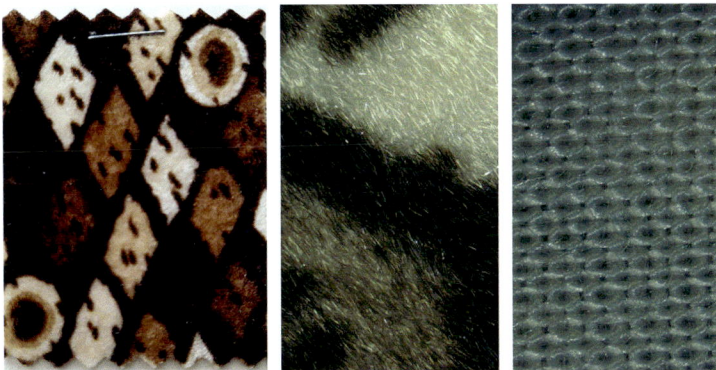

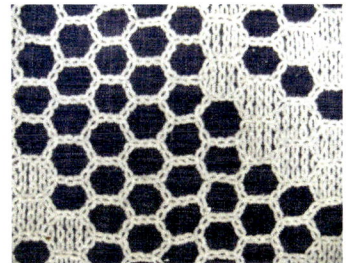

(*Top left*) Fig. 64. All-over flocked fabric with printed pattern; three views: front, close-up of flocks, close-up of the back. Photos taken by Margaret T. Ordoñez. Courtesy of Margaret T. Ordoñez's Sample Textile Collection.

(*Above*) Fig. 65. White flocking fibers adhered to blue woven fabric in a knitlike pattern. Photo taken by Kelly L. Reddy-Best. Courtesy of URI Textile Science Collection.

(*Bottom left*) Fig. 66. Flocking adhered to fabric to imitate clip-spot woven dotted swiss; flocks and adhesive are colored green. Four views: overall, close-up of fabric face, side, and back. Photos taken by Margaret T. Ordoñez. Courtesy of Margaret T. Ordoñez's Sample Textile Collection.

As the flock enter the electrical field they are polarized, take a vertical position, and fly up against the fabric with such force that they are embedded in the adhesive for about one-third of their length. They crowd so closely that from 250,000 to 300,000 flocks can be held by one square inch of the fabric, making a very thick pile. The flocks are cut from 0.02 to 0.07 inch long. From the electrodes the fabric passes to a curing oven, where the adhesive is hardened and the flock anchored. Possibilities in design are endless, and the process is much less expensive than pile formation by the usual method.[56]

Identification

If the back side of the fabric is accessible, look for flocked dots or patterns that will have adhesive visible on the back that would not be present in a woven backing. Sometimes the adhesive color provides a hue for white flocks. The back side of an all-over flock most likely will be a smooth, tightly woven plain weave, thinner than a pile weave with multiple sets of yarns.

Problems with Cleaning and Exhibiting Flocked Fabrics

Reports of flocked-fabric problems began in the late 1940s and continued until the end of the century. Flocked-fabric adhesives peeled, cracked, dissolved, stiffened, and caused partial or complete loss of flock due to the adhesive's solubility in water and solvent. Sometimes, problems occurred after only one commercial wet cleaning or dry cleaning. Fig. 67 illustrates pattern loss due to solvent solubility after one dry cleaning. Fig. 68 shows a sleeve with loss of flocked foam that peeled away from the base fabric after repeated dry cleanings. In the 1990s, retailers sold flocked draperies without care instructions because curtain and drapery materials were not covered under the Federal Trade Commission Care Label Rule. Some included care instructions printed on a hangtag, which consumers usually removed before use. [57]

The adhesives used on flocked draperies created considerable variance for serviceability. A 1992 *Clothes Care Gazette* bulletin reported that commercial wet cleaning and dry cleaning caused adhesive failure on curtains with tufts adhered to the surface. The solvent used during dry cleaning softened the adhesive under the fibers, resulting in a loss of pattern and surface distortion.

Flocked fabrics discolored, abraded, and distorted from the decomposition of adhesives over time. Starting in the 1960s, manufacturers adhered flock with neoprene, a synthetic adhesive that decomposed when exposed to the atmosphere. Neoprene contained a stabilizer to prevent it from decomposing or oxidizing; however, dry-cleaning solvent dissolved the stabilizer, and heat initialized the

Fig. 67. A flocked-stripe design. The adhesive binding the brown flocking fibers dissolved after one dry cleaning. Courtesy of DLI (*Fabric Facts*, April 1950).

Fig. 68. A coat constructed with flocked-foam fabric. The flocked foam on the coat sleeve peeled away from the base fabric during dry cleaning. Courtesy of DLI (*Fabric Facts*, October 1971).

disintegration. Neoprene contained chlorine, and when the adhesive broke down in the presence of moisture, it formed hydrochloric acid, which caused serious damage to adjacent fabrics.[58] As the adhesive decomposed over time, it also caused the flocked design to crack and break. Fig. 69 illustrates fabric damage from adhesive decomposition; the adhesive bonding the flock to the coat oxidized, which released acid, resulting in deterioration and a loss of strength. The adhesive bonding the flocked circles in Fig. 70 decomposed resulting in fabric degradation of the cotton organdy. After 1963, some flocking manufacturers switched to acrylic-based adhesives that were not affected by dry-cleaning solvents and did not break down or decompose like neoprene.

Exposure to light and abrasion also caused problems for flock adhesives. Minimal abrasion during handling and heavier abrasion during wear caused the flock to peel away from its base material. Aging and exposure to light discolored and yellowed synthetic-rubber binders.

Fig. 69. A flocked jacket. The neoprene adhesive used to bind the flock on the shoulders of the jacket oxidized, causing an acidic condition resulting in deterioration and loss of strength. Courtesy of DLI (*Fabric Facts*, June 1961).

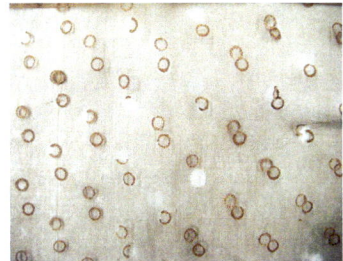

Fig. 70. A flocked-fabric sample. The adhesive bonding the flocking fibers caused fabric deterioration, creating holes in the sheer fabric. Photo taken by Kelly L. Reddy-Best. Courtesy of URI Textile Science Collection.

Recommendations for Cleaning, Storing, Handling, and Exhibiting Flocked Fabrics

- Avoid conservation wet cleaning or dry cleaning if a garment or object exhibits flock loss; cleaning most likely will increase the problem. Considering the frequency of adhesive failures starting in the 1940s, low-suction vacuuming, conservation wet cleaning, and dry cleaning all could result in additional loss.
- If a garment or object displays no obvious loss of flock, consider that adhesives often do not age well. Be careful in choosing to vacuum and conservation wet clean or dry clean.
- Maintain safe environmental conditions in storage, particularly humidity, to minimize adhesive decomposition. Closely monitor flocked garments, especially those from the 1960s, for deterioration or signs of loss. Once decomposition can be seen, isolate the garment and reconsider its value in the collection because it might cause damage to objects nearby in storage or on exhibition.
- Handle flocked fabrics with extreme caution while transporting and dressing mannequins. Avoid contact with other garments or objects in storage and on exhibition.
- Steam only if absolutely necessary, minimizing the amount of steam; test in an inconspicuous place, but be aware that areas of wear (collars, elbows, knees) could react differently than seam allowances. Avoid stressing flocked fabrics as garments are positioned and adjusted on mannequins.
- Keep light levels low and length of light exposure short during exhibition.

Chronology of Cleaning, Storing, and Exhibiting Problems for Flocked Fabrics

1946—Flock adhesives turned yellow when heat was applied.[59]

1949 –Rubber adhesives used for flocked stripes were not fast to dry cleaning.[60]

1950—Adhesives on some flocked fabrics dissolved in dry-cleaning solvent (Fig. 67).[61]

1958—Adhesives on some flocked fabrics dissolved in dry-cleaning solvent.[62]

1961—Flocking adhesive oxidized, causing an acidic condition resulting in loss of strength and deterioration (Fig. 69).[63]

1961—Light increased decomposition of synthetic binders holding flocking material to the base fabric.[64]

1961—Flock adhesives failed, and flocking fell off readily in areas exposed to abrasion during cleaning and wear.[65]

1961—Synthetic-rubber binding flocked suede decomposed over time when exposed to atmospheric gases causing strength loss. As the synthetic rubber decomposed, it formed hydrochloric acid.[66]

1963—Neoprene adhesives caused problems including discoloration, loss of flocking, and loss of strength.[67]

1971—Flocked foam peeled away from the base fabric during dry cleaning (Fig. 68).[68]

1973—Flocked material rubbed off during handling and cleaning.[69]

1975—Flocked fabrics had low resistance to edge abrasion.[70]

1976—Flocked fabrics lost flock during wear.[71]

1976—Flocked fabrics lost flock during commercial wet cleaning and dry cleaning.[72]

1976—Neoprene adhesives binding flocking material caused color change, loss of flock, loss of tensile strength, and stiffening of the base fabric.[73]

1988—Some adhesives used on flocked fabrics were soluble in dry-cleaning solvent.[74]

1992—Many flocked prints on formal attire lost flock after one cleaning.[75]

1992—Adhesives on flocked curtains failed during commercial wet cleaning and dry cleaning.[76]

1995—Dry cleaning solvent dissolved some bonding agents used on flocked fabrics causing the flock to separate, blister, and peel away from the base fabric.[77]

1999—Some patterned flocks lost their flock during dry cleaning because the adhesive dissolved in the solvent.[78]

Adhered Seams, Hems, and Pleats

Manufacturers traditionally stitched pleats, hems, and seams in garments, but some 1980s and 1990s producers replaced stitching with adhesives, which reduced production times and decreased labor costs.

Identification

The absence of sewing threads where they traditionally appear is a clue to suspect an adhesive connection. Pulling two fabrics apart, however, to identify the presence of an adhesive could weaken the support the adhesive provided.

Problems with Cleaning Adhered Seams, Hems, and Pleats

Adhesives securing pleats, hems, and seams dissolved during dry cleaning and commercial wet cleaning. Care labels instructed cleaners and consumers to dry clean some pleated bodices secured with an adhesive during 1958; however, the adhesive softened during dry cleaning, causing the pleats to sag and lose their sharpness. A 1993 bulletin reported that the adhesives used to bond hems and seams dissolved during dry cleaning, causing the seams and hems to open. After some adhesives softened, they leached out and stained the adjacent fabric.

Recommendations for Cleaning, Storing, Handling, and Exhibiting Adhered Seams, Hems, and Pleats

- Avoid dry cleaning and conservation wet cleaning if a garment has adhesive-held pleats, hems, or seams that have loosened because either treatment most likely will cause further damage.
- Due to infrequency of reported problems throughout the twentieth century, if a garment exhibits no evidence of damage and cleaning is necessary, test an adhered area in water or solvent before conservation wet cleaning or dry cleaning.
- In storage, minimize the number of folds in a garment with adhesive-held pleats, hems, or seams by selecting an appropriately sized box; pad fold lines.
- Handle gently in case the adhesive has weakened due to time, wear, or cleaning.
- Test an inconspicuous place to see how steam affects the adhesive; minimize the amount of steam and hold the steam nozzle at least 12 inches from the garment so the steam is cool and wet.
- Do not stress adhered seams, hems, and pleats while handling and dressing mannequins.

Fig. 71. Dress with an adhered hem tape that partially detached during dry cleaning. The solvent dissolved the adhesive coating, releasing the hem tape from the fabric. Courtesy of DLI (Lyle, *Focus on Fabrics*, 514).

Chronology of Cleaning Problems for Adhered Seams, Hems, and Pleats

1958—Pleated inserts of dresses secured with an adhesive lost their sharpenss due to the adhesives' dissolving in dry-cleaning solvent.[79]

1958—Dry-cleaning solvent dissolved the adhesive on the hem tape, causing it to detach from the fabric (Fig. 71).[80]

1988—Adhesive used to secure a pleated bodice insert dissolved in dry-cleaning solvent, causing pleats to loosen from garment and hang down.[81]

1993—Adhesives bonding seams or hems were not resistant to commercial wet cleaning and dry cleaning and stained adjacent fabric.[82]

Bonded-Wool Shoulder Pads and Quilted Linings

Manufacturers in the early 1950s made inexpensive shoulder pads by bonding wool, foam, and nonwoven materials with neoprene, a synthetic rubber. In 1955, some of them changed the formulation to reduce acid formation; however, others still continued to use the problematic formulas. Later in the decade, linings that incorporated neoprene-bonded wool significantly degraded adjacent fabrics. Then neoprene-bonded wool shoulder pads reappeared in the mid-1990s and created the same problems as before. Adjacent degraded fabrics became apparent when the garments were dry cleaned.

Identification

Bonded-wool shoulder pads probably have covers, and quilted linings of bonded-wool interlining also will be multilayer. The nonwoven structure of the interior will be wool fibers stuck together with an adhesive. Look for discoloration and degradation of fabrics adjacent to shoulder pads or interlining. Damage suggests the presence of aging adhesives in the bonded wool. An odor also is an indication of bonded-wool components.

Problems with Cleaning, Storing, and Exhibiting Bonded-Wool Shoulder Pads and Quilted Linings

The Drycleaning and Laundry Institute International (DLI) bulletins in the 1950s reported problems that became apparent when cleaning garments with neoprene-bonded-wool shoulder pads and neoprene-bonded-wool interlinings. The problems with wool-bonded shoulder pads reccurred in the mid-1990s. The neoprene adhesive degraded and released hydrochloric acid that leached out of the shoulder pads

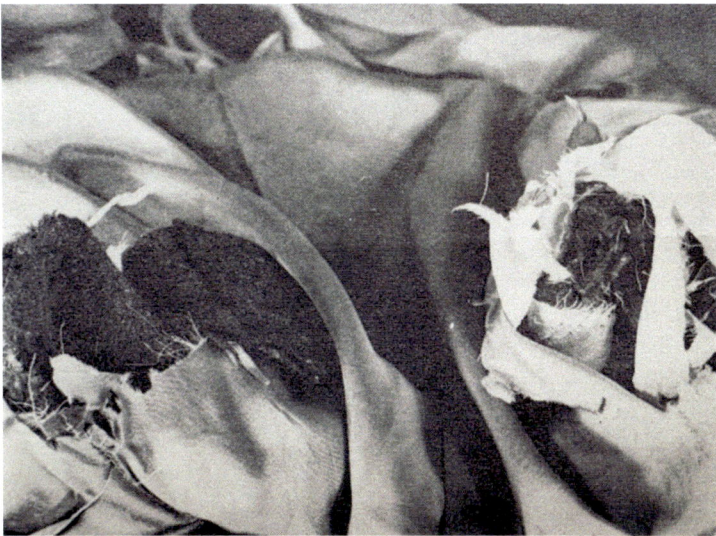

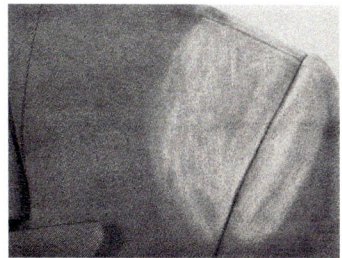

(*Above*) Fig. 72. A jacket with degraded neoprene bonded-wool shoulder pads. The bonded-wool shoulder pad degraded and discolored the outer fabric of the jacket. Courtesy of DLI (*Fabric Facts*, August 1951).

(*Above left*) Fig. 73. Close-up of a jacket with degraded bonded-wool shoulder pads. Breakdown of the neoprene adhesive in the shoulder pads on the jacket deteriorated the adjacent fabric. Photo courtesy of DLI (*Fabric Facts*, August 1951).

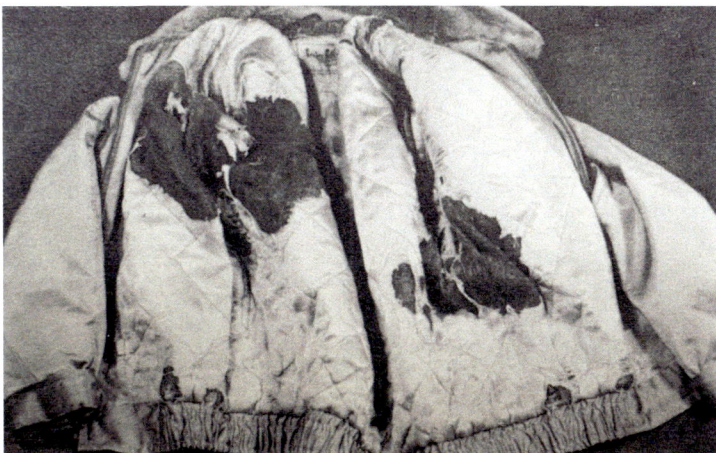

(*Below left*) Fig. 74. A jacket with a degraded quilted lining. The jacket's neoprene-bonded-wool insulating layer caused the disintegration. Courtesy of DLI (*Fabric Facts*, February 1957).

Fig. 75. Damage to degraded outer fabric in the jacket with a neoprene-bonded wool quilted lining in Fig. 74. Courtesy of DLI (*Fabric Facts*, February 1957).

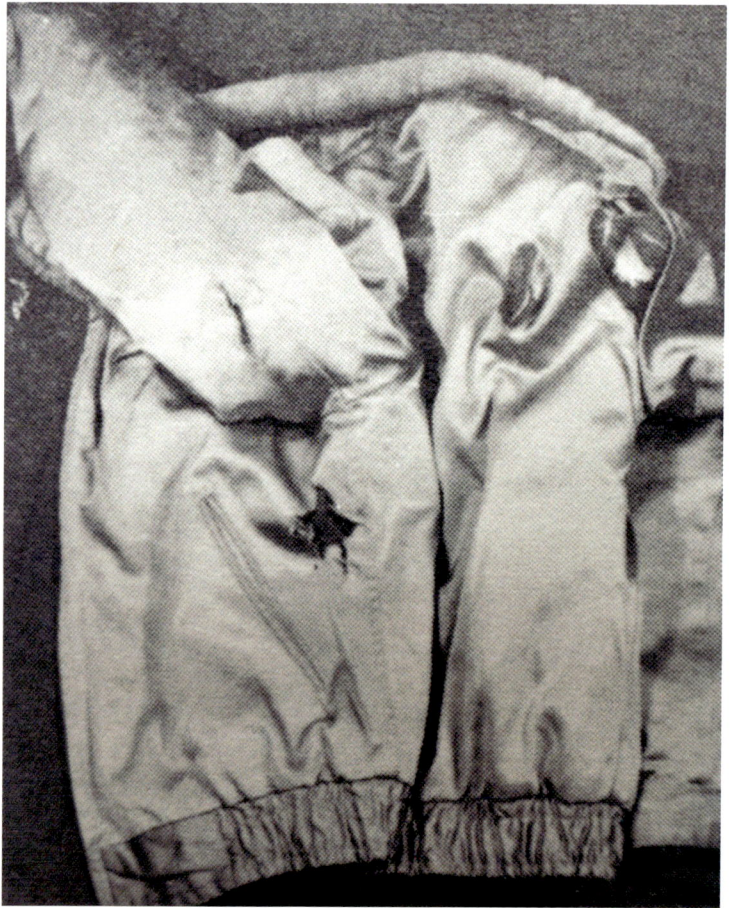

and interlinings, staining and degrading adjacent fabrics. Fig. 72 shows typical color loss in the shape of the shoulder pad on the outer fabric. Figs. 73, 74, and 75 show deterioration of fabrics adjacent to neoprene-bonded wool.

Recommendations for Cleaning, Storing, Handling, and Exhibiting Bonded-Wool Shoulder Pads and Quilted Linings

- Do not conservation wet clean or dry clean garments with bonded-wool components dating from the 1950s and the mid-1990s.
- Examine all garments with shoulder pads from the fifties and nineties to identify those made of bonded wool. Document, photograph, and remove potentially harmful shoulder pads; if a garment has excessive fabric decomposition similar to those in Figs. 73, 74, and 75, consider deaccessioning.
- Do not steam the shoulder area of garments where fabrics could have been affected by the shoulder pads; steam will accelerate migration of the hydrochloric acid from the neoprene.

- Replace stiffened shoulder pads in exhibit preparation to create a proper silhouette and prevent damage to adjacent fabrics.

Chronology of Cleaning and Exhibiting Problems for Bonded-Wool Shoulder Pads and Quilted Linings

1951—Some shoulder pads adhered with neoprene broke down and stained outer fabric (Fig. 72).[83]

1951—Some bonded-wool shoulder pads gave off hydrochloric acid strongly enough to change the color of the dyestuffs and degrade adjacent materials (Fig. 73).[84]

1955—Some bonded-wool shoulder pads broke down and gave off hydrochloric acid, disintegrating the adjacent suit.[85]

1957—Bonded wool in a quilted coat lining contained neoprene, which deteriorated over time, changing the color and deteriorating adjacent fabrics.[86]

1958—Bonded wool, adhered with neoprene, produced enough acid to change the color of some dyes on adjacent linings and outer fabrics (Fig. 76).[87]

1995—The adhesive used to construct some shoulder pads dissolved during dry cleaning and stained outer fabric.[88]

1996—Some nonwoven shoulder pads' adhesives dissolved during dry cleaning, causing stiff brown stains on outer fabric.[89]

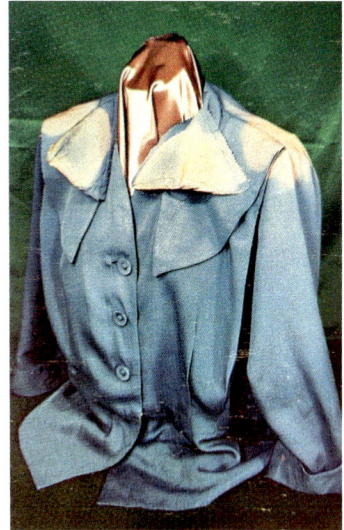

Fig. 76. A jacket with degraded bonded-wool shoulder pads that was folded while in storage. Color change in the fabric was caused by hydrochloric acid from the neoprene binder in the shoulder pads. Courtesy of DLI (Lyle, *Focus on Fabrics*, 380).

6 Finishes

During the twentieth century, research-and-development departments worked to improve the appearance, performance, hand, and texture of fabrics. Mechanical manipulation or the application of a chemical altered their aesthetics and performance. Manufacturers applied durable, semidurable, or nondurable finishes, modifying formulas and procedures to improve customer satisfaction of newly introduced products. Sometimes labels reflected changes, but often consumers did not know when adjustments occurred. This also presents a problem for collection caretakers' expectations and choice of treatment today. The fabric of two similar garments made a few months apart can age and react quite differently.

Chintz Fabrics

In the twentieth century, manufacturers produced nondurable and durable glazed finishes on chintz fabrics for apparel and home furnishings (Fig. 77). They pressed wax and starch into the fabrics with hot rollers to produce a high-luster, nondurable-chintz finish and later treated fabrics with urea or melamine resins to produce durable-chintz finishes. The first durable type distributed in the United States was sold beginning in 1939 under the trade name Everglaze.

Identification

Chintzes are printed or solid-colored, plain-weave cotton fabrics with a glossy, flattened surface on one side. If a chintz must be cleaned and a small sample of the fabric can be obtained, clean it to determine the durability of the finish. A wax or starch finish will wash off and leave a dull, fuzzy surface.

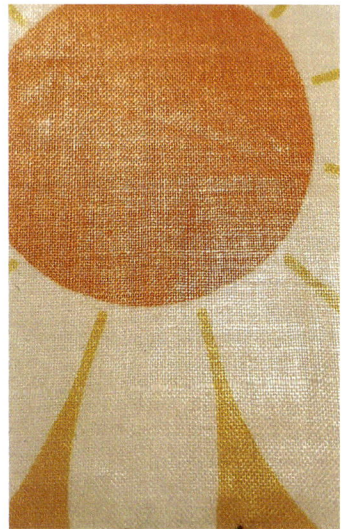

Fig. 77. Chintz-treated printed plain-weave cotton fabric, circa 1978. Photo taken by Margaret T. Ordoñez. Courtesy of Margaret T. Ordoñez's Sample Textile Collection.

Problems with Cleaning Chintz Fabrics

The nondurable finishes are not limited to the first forty years of the century. They are not permanent and can be removed with detergent or solvent. Three reports during the 1970s, 1980s, and 1990s documented chintz problems. Dry cleaning and professional wet cleaning partially removed starch-glaze finishes.

Recommendations for Cleaning, Storing, Handling, and Exhibiting Chintz Fabrics

- Be cautious in dry cleaning or conservation wet cleaning chintz fabrics: both methods will reduce or possibly remove a non- or semipermanent glaze. See identification section above for testing the permanence of a finish.
- Be aware that over time wax and starch in a chintz fabric will age, become acidic, and discolor, often yellowing and stiffening the fabric.
- Store chintz fabrics with as few folds as possible; pad fold lines; rolling flat pieces of chintz fabric on an acid-free tube eliminates folds; place acid-free tissue between layers of fabrics.
- Minimize pressure on folds when handling chintz fabric.
- Humidify creases by steaming the back side of the fabric and applying pressure to flatten the fabric or by sandwiching a flat chintz fabric between slightly dampened blotter paper held in place by weights. Lessen creases in three-dimensional garments by holding slightly damp blotter paper on the back of the fabric until humidity is increased sufficiently to relax the deformation.

Chronology of Cleaning Problems for Chintz Fabrics

Prior to 1939—Professional wet cleaning removed nonpermanent-glaze finishes.[1]

1958—Fabrics with a heavily applied finish developed white streaks when bent or flexed in use and cleaning; no method to overcome this damage was known.[2]

1975—Dry cleaning and professional wet cleaning caused loss of finish, altered the hand, and produced a dulled and streaked appearance on chintz fabrics.[3]

1989—Dry cleaning and professional wet cleaning removed some chintz finishes.[4]

1990—Dry cleaning and professional wet cleaning removed finishes on Everglaze chintz-treated fabrics, leaving the fabric limp and altering the textured appearance.[5]

Ciré Fabrics

A "brilliant patent leather effect" characterized ciré fabrics.[6] At the beginning of the century, manufacturers applied wax to a fabric, then calendared it, to produce a smooth lustrous surface on silk and rayon fabrics. After 1938, synthetic resins applied to fabrics of both natural and heat-setting synthetic fibers made the finish permanent, although some manufacturers continued to use wax and starch to produce a shiny ciré effect. While the fabric was used chiefly for evening wear, it made a major fashion statement with the wet look of the 1960s.[7]

Identification

Ciré fabrics have a glossy smooth surface on one side. The coating on the fabric is apparent. The surface of a polyvinyl chloride–resin-coated fabric may feel waxy, and the fabric has a distinctive smell, like new PVC gloves.

Problems with Cleaning and Storing Ciré Fabrics

A wax finish is not durable and can be removed by wet or dry cleaning. Heat turned some wax finishes brown. Professional wet cleaning removed some ciré finishes, leaving the fabrics distorted. Folding and twisting ciré-finished fabrics left the garments with permanent white streaks or marks. The use of PVC resin to produce ciré effects, however, presents a potential problem with storage and exhibition, especially the 1960s' *wet-look* coats, garments, and accessories (boots, belts, hats, and bags).

Recommendations for Cleaning, Storing, Handling, and Exhibiting Ciré Fabrics

- Be cautious in dry cleaning or conservation wet cleaning ciré fabrics. These treatments could reduce or remove the finish, which cannot be replaced. Test an inconspicuous area with water and solvent for finish solubility.
- Store ciré garments on a padded hanger or flat with as few folds as possible; pad fold lines.
- Minimize pressure on folds when handling ciré fabrics.
- Be cautious when steaming; if steaming is necessary, test in an inconspicuous area first; applying steam to the back side of the fabric will effectively relax creases more than steaming the front.
- See chapter 4 for recommendations for cleaning, exhibiting, storing, and handling PVC-coated fabrics from the 1960s to the end of the century (50–53).

1923—Heat turned wax finishes brown.[8]
1935—Wet cleaning dissolved and distorted many ciré finishes.[9]
1936—Professional wet cleaning dissolved some ciré finishes.[10]
1974—Folding and twisting ciré-finished fabrics caused permanent white streaks and marks.[11]

Moiré Fabrics

The wavy rippling pattern in moiré fabrics has been popular since the eighteenth century. Traditionally, manufacturers produced them by running a ribbed fabric, folded lengthwise with the ribs face-to-face, under pressure between rollers, flattening portions of the ribs and causing differential light reflectance (Fig. 78). This mechanical finish technique created the traditional moiré finish with a wood-grain or watered effect, also referred to as "antique moiré." In the 1940s, manufacturers also reproduced the effect by running a resin-treated cotton, silk, rayon, or a thermoplastic fabric under a roller engraved with a moiré pattern. The latter was characterized by a repeated motif pattern in a 15- to 18-inch repeat, while the former had a constantly changing pattern.[12] Throughout the century, some European manufacturers continued to use the traditional method of producing the pattern, which is less permanent.[13]

Identification

If a small sample of the fabric can be obtained, wet it with a detergent solution to determine whether the characteristic moiré pattern is diminished. If so, it is a traditionally produced moiré or a nonpermanent resin. The presence of a center-fold line also is a clue to the traditional method.

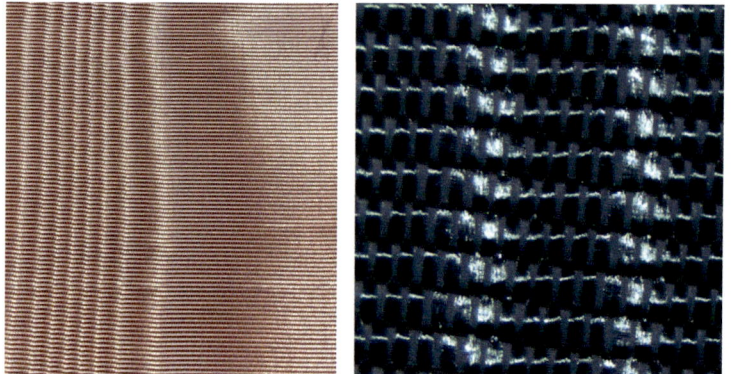

Fig. 78. Traditionally produced moiré fabric; two views: front, with a pattern of wavy lines, and a close-up, showing the flattened yarns that appear shiny. Photos taken by Margaret T. Ordoñez. Courtesy of Margaret T. Ordoñez's Sample Textile Collection.

Problems with Cleaning, Exhibiting, and Storing Moiré Fabrics

The moiré patterns created by the traditional pressure-roller method are less permanent than those set with an engraved resin; they are sensitive to moisture. The centerfold crease produced in creating the pattern also is more likely to have yarn damage along the crease than the resin-treated fabrics, which are finished as a single layer. Professional wet cleaning increased the likelihood of damage to moiré fabrics produced with the engraved-roller method. Sometimes an error occurred in the mechanical process and produced an imperfection in the fabric design. When the roller pressure was not carefully controlled, the sharp edges of the raised-roller design cut the yarns, increasing damage probability during handling, use, and cleaning.

Recommendations for Cleaning, Storing, Handling, and Exhibiting Moiré Fabrics

- Vacuum using low suction in the warp direction and with no surface abrasion.
- Be aware that if a moiré fabric must be wet cleaned, a detergent solution could relax the fibers, and the moiré effect will be reduced; if a small sample can be obtained, wet it to determine the durability of the finish before conservation wet cleaning.
- Remove oily soil on moiré fabric by dry cleaning with minimal agitation, but steaming afterward should be limited.
- Examine a moiré fabric for evidence of weakened yarns along the fold line created during traditional production as well as roller damage before choosing treatment.
- Store moiré fabrics and garments with as few folds as possible; pad fold lines.
- Limit the amount of steam applied to a ribbed weave with a moiré finish.

Chronology of Cleaning Problems for Moiré Fabrics

1938—Professional wet cleaning partially faded permanent moiré designs on acetate fabrics.[14]

1955—Professional wet cleaning increased damage incurred during production of moiré fabrics.[15]

1958—Cleaning damaged moiré fabrics because engraving rollers cut the yarns of the fabric during manufacture; cleaning increased loosening of cut fibers from yarns (Fig. 79).[16]

1958—Professional wet cleaning and dry cleaning distorted and faded moiré designs.[17]

1966—Professional wet cleaning distorted and faded moiré designs.[18]

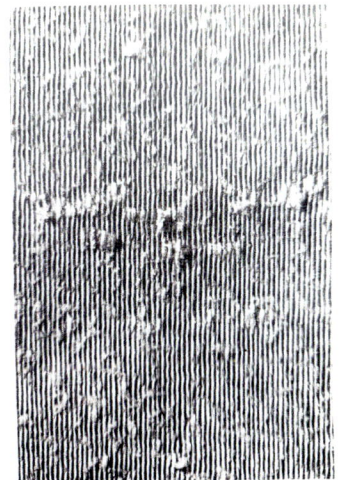

Fig. 79. Moiré design on an embossed bengaline. The engraving rollers that created the moiré design on the embossed bengaline cut the yarns; wet cleaning frayed them. Courtesy of Drycleaning and Laundry Institute International (DLI) (Lyle, *Focus on Fabrics*, 443).

1987—Professional wet cleaning and steaming removed moiré designs on fabrics of non-thermoplastic fibers.[19]

1989—The engraved rollers used during manufacture initially cut the yarns on moiré fabrics, and professional wet cleaning caused further damage and fraying on the surface.[20]

1990—Professional wet cleaning and dry cleaning increased distortion and damage of moiré fabrics because engraving rollers cut and damaged the yarns of moiré fabric during manufacture.[21]

Fabrics with Sizings

Sizings form continuous solid films around yarns and individual fibers. Manufacturers applied them to yarns or fabrics to increase smoothness, abrasion resistance, body, strength, weight, and luster. Starches, waxes, resins, and synthetic polymers, such as polyvinyl alcohol, created a special surface effect or increased body.[22]

Identification

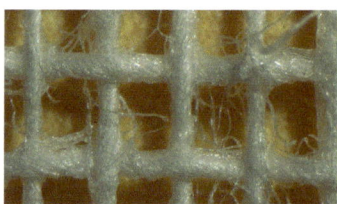

Fig. 80. Close-up of a starch finish on cotton yarns of a 1973 crinoline (open-weave) fabric to add stiffness. Photo taken by Margaret T. Ordoñez. Courtesy of Margaret McWilliams. Swatch 72 in Joseph and Gieseking, *Illustrated Guide to Textiles*.

Sizing often makes a fabric noticeably stiffer and is microscopically visible as a coating on the fibers and yarns in a fabric (Fig. 80). Starch (glucose) is a common nonpermanent sizing material and can be identified by applying a tincture of iodine to unraveled yarns or an inconspicuous spot that turns blue if starch is present. Warning: the blue color is permanent. Early sizing formulations also included wax and gelatin, also not permanent.

Problems with Cleaning, Exhibiting, and Storing Fabrics with Sizings

Dry cleaning, professional wet cleaning, and steaming created problems for some sizings on woven fabrics and net. The fabrics distorted and appeared limp after cleaning or steaming. Sizings often softened and dissolved during cleaning, leaving a significantly altered, distorted, and limp appearance. Some sizings that softened in water migrated, creating dark-shaded spots, as shown in Fig. 81.[23]

Fig. 81. Sized fabric. Water softened the sizing on the fabric, causing it to migrate to one area and create dark stains. Courtesy of DLI (*TABS*, 1988).

Recommendations for Cleaning, Storing, Handling, and Exhibiting Fabrics with Sizings

- Test all fabrics for sizing solubility in water or solvent before cleaning, unless the goal is to remove yellowed, oxidized starch or wax; be aware that the removal of sizing will result in a loss of body, producing a limp fabric.

- Fold stiffly starched fabrics and garments that are stored flat as few times as possible; pad folds to lessen the stresses created by bending stiff fabric.
- Be aware that starch discolors as it ages and can be a food source for silverfish and fungi; monitor garments and accessories for these conditions.
- Minimize pressure on folds when handling fabrics stiff with sizing.
- Be aware that steaming starched cotton or linen fabric seldom removes wrinkles and can cause sizings to migrate; if wrinkles or creases must be lessened or removed, use a steam iron and a pressing cloth after testing in an inconspicuous area.
- Avoid steaming heavily sized nets and fabrics to prevent layers from sticking together when damp.
- Be aware that fabrics with sizing might have a low fabric count (number of warps and wefts) and thus low strength; provide proper support in storage and exhibition.

Chronology of Cleaning and Exhibiting Problems for Fabrics with Sizings

1923—Steaming distorted starched fabrics.[24]

1923—Maline—a stiff silk net with a hexagonal pattern used in veils, millinery, and dress trimming—became gummy with moisture; manufacturers applied a treatment to help it withstand moisture.[25]

1950—Dry cleaning softened sizing on net portions of gowns, leaving the fabric bunched and distorted and the surface sticky.[26]

1952—Dry cleaning significantly changed the dimensions of sized taffeta fabrics.[27]

1956—Professional wet cleaning and dry cleaning dissolved sizings on taffeta fabrics, leaving the fabrics limp.[28]

1956—Dry cleaning, professional wet cleaning, and steaming dissolved sizings used on taffeta fabrics.[29]

1958—Professional wet cleaning dissolved sizings on net fabrics, leaving them limp and distorted.[30]

1984—Agitation during professional wet cleaning and dry cleaning softened sizings, allowing the fabric to relax.[31]

1988—Some sizings softened in water and migrated to one area, creating dark-shaded spots (Fig. 81).[32]

1989—Steaming dissolved heavy application of sizings on wedding dresses, permanently altering appearance and texture of the fabrics.[33]

1990—Dry cleaning softened sizings, leaving the fabric limp.[34]

Fabrics with Wrinkle-Resistant Finishes

At the beginning of the century, applying nondurable starch to a fabric followed by ironing reduced wrinkling and produced a smooth finish. Around 1930, chemists started researching resin-finishing processes to overcome the tendency of cellulosic-fiber fabrics to wrinkle during everyday use. Urea formaldehyde-resin finishes, patented in 1929, began the succession of synthetic wrinkle-resistant finishes for cotton, linen, and rayon fabrics. The initial synthetic finishes successfully resisted wrinkles but had many weaknesses, which furthered continuous research and development for the rest of the century. From the 1930s onward, urea formaldehyde-finished textiles discolored (yellowed), weakened the fabric, and developed a fishy odor when enclosed in storage due to the release of formaldehyde.

Debates from the 1960s onward addressed health dangers associated with formaldehyde levels in the finishes. In the 1980s, dimethylo-dihydroxyethyleneurea formed the base of most wrinkle-free finishes, and by the end of the century, research moved toward ultra-low formaldehyde levels in fabrics. Zero-formaldehyde finishes became available but were more expensive.[35] The treated cotton fabrics often suffered from a decrease in tensile strength, tear strength, abrasion resistance, and sewability, with a stiff, harsh, and uncomfortable feel.

Wrinkle-resistant finishes applied to cellulosic fabrics reduced wrinkling and increased wrinkle recovery, but they prevented the retention of sharp creases in garments made of the fabric. Pants and pleated skirts did not retain their creases when laundered. Solving this problem resulted in a "post-cure" process that fixed the finish on completed garments rather than flat fabric.[36] The new durable-press finish increased garment performance by providing shape retention, durable creases and pleats, durably smooth seams, machine wash and dry, and fresh appearance without ironing.[37] The processes that followed varied the wrinkle-resistant finish formulations and applications for decades in response to consumer feedback, contributing to inconsistent performance, smoothness, and permanence. Terms for wrinkle-resistant finishes included *wash-and-wear, easy care, durable press,* and *permanent press.*[38] Wrinkle-resistant finishes are a good example of research-and-development departments adjusting formulations over time.

Identification

If signs of degradation that are typical of wrinkle-resistant finishes are absent (see below), the amount of wrinkling and creasing in an object's fabric might be a clue to identifying the presence of a finish. A noticeable formaldehyde-like odor confirms that a fabric has a wrinkle-resistant finish.

Problems with Cleaning, Exhibiting, and Storing Fabrics with Wrinkle-Resistant Finishes

Reported wrinkle-resistant-finish problems began in 1957 and continued frequently to the end of the century. Professional wet cleaning and dry cleaning as well as home laundering damaged the finished fabrics, as did wear and time. Over time, the finishes stiffened, decomposed, and contributed to significant strength loss of the fabrics.

Abrasion on the collars and cuffs of men's shirts, knees of children's pants, and hems of men's pants often showed fraying and frosting, a color change that resulted from the breakage and loss of fibers due to abrasion, exposing undyed yarns (Fig. 82). The fibers' soft, fuzzy ends gave abraded areas a lighter or darker shade of color, depending on the color of the synthetic fibers that had not worn away in blended fabrics.[39]

Heat from steam and high water temperatures caused fabric discoloration and yellowing. Professional wet cleaning caused the fabrics to shrink, seams to pucker, and cuffs to fade and frost. Dry cleaning caused the fabrics to split. Some cotton fabrics with a durable-press finish underwent strength loss as high as 50 percent during dry cleaning.

Fig. 82. Pants with a wrinkle-resistant finish. The wrinkle-resistant finish caused loss of strength, resulting in frosting at the crease and fraying along the pant hem. Photo taken by Martin Bide. Courtesy of Martin Bide's Personal Collection.

Recommendations for Cleaning, Storing, Handling, and Exhibiting Fabrics with Wrinkle-Resistant Finishes

- Due to the high frequency of problems, carefully consider any cleaning treatments.
- Use minimal agitation in any cleaning treatments.
- Isolate fabrics emitting bad odors; consider deaccessioning.
- Handle and move garments with care to avoid stressing, abrading, frosting, or fraying the fabrics.
- Use a steam iron and a pressing cloth to reduce wrinkles after testing in an inconspicuous area; stop ironing if fabric begins to emit an odor or change color.
- Access the condition of the fabric in a garment to be displayed and provide adequate support based on the fabric's strength.

Chronology of Cleaning, Exhibiting, and Storing Problems for Fabrics with Wrinkle-Resistant Finishes

1957—Professional wet cleaning caused excessive shrinkage on crease-resistant-finished cotton garments.[40]

1959—Wash-and-wear finishes reduced strength of shirt fabrics, causing abrasion at collar points, pockets, and cuffs.[41]

1962—Formaldehyde resins broke down and released irritating fumes and intense odors.[42]

1962—Some crease-resistant finishes stiffened fabrics over time.[43]

1963—Seams puckered after cleaning wash-and-wear-treated fabric.[44]

1964—Dry cleaning split and weakened formaldehyde-treated fabrics.[45]

1965—Components of some permanent-press treatments sublimed when heated and turned yellow.[46]

1965—Professional wet cleaning discolored and faded dark-colored fabrics treated with a permanent-press finish.[47]

1967—Professional wet cleaning puckered seams on wash-and-wear-treated cotton blouses.[48]

1968–78—Professional wet cleaning caused frosted and frayed cuffs on polyester and cotton–blended, dark-colored, durable-press-treated men's shirts.[49]

1980—Durable press finishes, which used a delayed cure process, slowly decomposed fabrics because of an acid salt used as a catalyst during curing.[50]

1988—Professional wet cleaning caused severe tensile-strength loss of lightweight, wrinkle-resistant cellulosic fabrics, resulting in holes.[51]

1988—Some wrinkle-resistant finishes caused severe loss of strength and abrasion resistance on lightweight-cellulosic fabrics especially around the lapels, cuff edges, points of pockets, and hems (Fig. 82).[52]

1995—Wrinkle-resistant finishes stiffened fabrics.[53]

1997—Durable-press finishes decreased abrasion resistance, causing fraying and frosting on men's shirts and children's clothing.[54]

Fabrics with Water-Repellent and Waterproof Finishes

Throughout the century, a variety of materials produced waterproof coatings on fabrics, closing the interstices between the yarns and allowing no water to penetrate the cloth. Water-repellent fabrics repelled water yet were not entirely waterproof. This finish allowed air passage, increasing comfort, as opposed to waterproof finishes that made fabric airtight and uncomfortable. Scientists developed many chemical approaches to provide water repellency, including rubber solutions, wax emulsions, resin mixtures, metallic soaps, silicones, fluorocarbons, and various other hydrophobic finishes.[55] The first three of these, in particular, might not age well, stiffening or producing an odor.

Identification

Water repellency can be determined easily by placing a drop of water on the surface of a fabric in an inconspicuous place and observing whether the water is absorbed within a short period of time. The method used to produce water resistance is not as easily identified, but undesirable characteristics include an odor, discoloration, stiffening, stickiness, and cracking.

Problems with Cleaning Fabrics with Water-Repellent and Waterproof Finishes

In the 1950s and 1970s, bulletins reported two problems for water-repellent finishes. Dry cleaning and professional wet cleaning removed some water-repellent finishes, changing the function and appearance of the fabric as well as increasing limpness. Dry cleaning also stiffened some waterproof-finished fabrics.

Recommendations for Cleaning, Storing, Handling, and Exhibiting Fabrics with Water-Repellent and Waterproof Finishes

- Consider whether preserving the finish is more important than removal of soil; clean as necessary for type of soil.
- Limit cleaning to low-suction vacuuming and wiping surface with slightly damp cloth if the fabric is altered, stiff, or limp.
- Isolate the object if undesirable characteristics such as an odor or stickiness has developed; avoid using tissue paper or cloth to cover a fabric with a sticky surface and use silicone-release paper instead. Consider deaccessioning if undesirable characteristics include an odor, discoloration, stiffening, stickiness, or cracking.
- Limit the number of folds in an object that has become stiff or if the surface coating is stiffened when storing in a box; pad the necessary folds.
- Avoid creasing a fabric that has a stiffened or cracking surface coating; limit handling if the surface is sticky.
- Limit steaming; if reducing wrinkles and creases is absolutely necessary, use cool steam (hold source of steam 12 or more inches away) on the inside of the fabric.
- Avoid stressing the fabric when dressing a mannequin; provide sufficient support to garments or accessories on display.

Chronology of Cleaning Problems for Fabrics with Water-Repellent and Waterproof Finishes

1953—Dry cleaning and professional wet cleaning removed some water-repellent finishes.[56]
1976—Dry cleaning stiffened waterproof-finished fabrics.[57]

7 Plastics

In the early twentieth century, garment, accessory, and adornment manufacturers began replacing a number of traditional natural materials with semisynthetic and synthetic plastics due to their relative inexpensiveness. The Great International Exhibition of 1862 showcased the first cellulose-nitrate-based plastic, a completely new product based on the chemical modification of cellulose. The addition of plasticizers transformed cellulose nitrate into a moldable and flexible material. Also in the early twentieth century, manufacturers developed cellulose acetate, which became commercially available in 1918 and became the major molded thermoplastic for buttons, sequins, other adornments, and accessories.[1]

Research into the development of new plastics began in the 1920s and accelerated between 1935 and 1945; World War II restrictions on importation of raw materials prompted research. Scientists began investigating polyvinyl chloride (PVC) in the 1920s, yet its successful commercial availability did not start until 1942. Otto Bayer and his team began work on polyurethane polymers in 1937, and the accidental introduction of water to the reaction mix created flexible polyurethane foams, commercially available in the 1950s.[2] The cutoff of rubber imports during the war spurred the use of polyurethane and drove polystyrene's entrance into commercial availability around 1948, although scientists had begun molding trials in the 1930s. In the 1950s, plastics significantly increased in use. By the 1990s, manufacturers marketed over fifty types of plastics, although the consumers seldom knew the composition.[3]

As synthetic and semisynthetic plastics developed, manufacturers molded the new materials into buttons, beads, sequins, buckles, hatpin heads, costume jewelry, purse clasps, shoe ornaments, eyeglass frames, and combs. Accessories such as vanity sets and shoehorns also incorporated plastics, and some textile and apparel collections may include these objects.

Plastics reduced production costs by replacing more expensive natural materials, such as pearl and ivory. Polymers molded into useful shapes commonly needed additives to give them color, stability, strength, and processability; these additives complicated the reaction of polymers to wearing, cleaning, and aging. Consumers and commercial cleaners were ill-informed about plastic products' serviceability. Despite the permanent-care labeling legislation of 1972, some manufacturers added plastic to garments after serviceability testing on fabrics, which led to inaccurate care labels. Contemporary reports seldom addressed degradation of twentieth-century plastics, but conservation literature covers these problems in depth.[4] "For certain categories of plastics—in particular, the cellulose esters [cellulose nitrate and cellulose acetate], polyurethane, and plasticized PVC—the alarm bells undoubtedly are justified. Objects made of these compounds often quickly exhibit severe symptoms of degradation, such as discoloration, embrittlement, distortion, cracking, stickiness, or the reek of vinegar or vomit."[5]

Cellulose-Nitrate Accessories

Cellulose nitrate—also referred to as *nitrocellulose* and *guncotton*, as well as the brand names Celluloid, Collodion, Ivoride, Parkesine, Pyralin, Pyroxylin, and Xylonite was first used in photography in the 1840s. Alexander Parkes nitrated cellulose, a natural polymer in wood and cotton, with a mixture of nitric and sulfuric acids to make cellulose nitrate. By adding a solvent, he produced moldable products that he patented as Parkesine and displayed at the 1862 International Exhibition in London. Daniel Spill continued his former employer's work in 1869; his Xylonite Company marketed products labeled Xylonite and Ivoride, particularly imitating ivory and tortoiseshell. Parks, Spill, and American John Wesley Hyatt had experimented with adding camphor to cellulose nitrate as a solvent and plasticizer; in 1870 Hyatt patented this modification to Parkes's original work and named the product *celluloid;* in 1872 he established the Celluloid Manufacturing Company. By the 1880s, celluloid use in novelties and fancy goods was well established: "Items made of celluloid were very popular with the era's growing middle class."[6] Celluloid replaced cotton fabric for men's detachable shirt collars and cuffs. The 1899 Xylonite Company catalog listed 1100 celluloid-containing items.[7] That company and the Celluloid Manufacturing Company, both under various owners, continued production of cellulose-nitrate products that could be in apparel and accessory collections today. These products include jewelry, buttons, belt buckles, beads, sequins, heads of hat pins, picture frames, vanity sets, watch chains, eyeglass frames, fake leather, mirror frames, shoes, shoehorns, walking-cane handles, dolls, and toys.[8] The materials often imitated were ivory, amber, coral, tortoise shell, carnelian, shell, and lacquered beads.[9]

Identification

By the twenty-first century, most cellulose-nitrate objects have begun to show some signs of decomposition. An odor of camphor or naphtha, added as a plasticizer in the manufacturing process, is an excellent clue. Another definite identifying feature of degrading cellulose nitrate is the formation of crystals within an object's structure. Fig. 83 illustrates a cracked and discolored belt buckle with well-developed crystal formation, one of the last degradation steps before the object's total loss of integrity. Discoloration of adjacent metal components and degradation of paper used to wrap an object are additional signs of aging cellulose nitrate.[10]

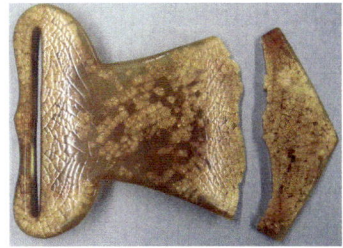

Fig. 83. Circa 1920s cellulose-nitrate belt buckle that shows late-stage degradation. Photo taken by Kelly L. Reddy-Best. Courtesy of University of Rhode Island (URI) Textile Conservation Collection.

Problems with Cleaning, Exhibiting, and Storing Cellulose-Nitrate Accessories

Early cellulose-nitrate contained camphor, a plasticizer used to soften the plastic. Its properties created two disadvantages for cellulose nitrate's aging stability. Impurities in camphor caused cellulose nitrate to yellow or discolor the originally clear plastics. Also, camphor sublimed at room temperature. Low camphor levels resulted in cracks and increased brittleness.[11]

Over time, cellulose-nitrate objects discolor, crack, craze, weep, warp, crumble, embrittle, bloom, and develop a mothball or acidic smell.[12] They can emit corrosive gases for many years before a noticeable odor or cracks occur. Acid produced by the degradation also tarnishes and corrodes nearby metals and degrades fabrics and leather. Cellulose nitrate inherently deteriorates; however, moisture, heat, light, and exposure to atmospheric fumes significantly accelerate degradation. Humidity and light make the greatest contribution to the rate of acid degradation. Limited ventilation increases embrittlement and decomposition, damaging the plastic and neighboring objects.[13] Paradichlorobenzene (mothballs) also increases the degradation of cellulose nitrate.

Figs. 84–87 exhibit various degrading twentieth-century cellulose-nitrate objects. The belt buckle in Fig. 84 shows crystal formation in its cellulose-nitrate backing in Fig. 85. Figs. 86 and 87 exhibit excessive degradation. The pre-1940 purse handle cracked and crumbled, and it still weeps onto the tissue paper with which it is wrapped. The nitric acid that formed during decomposition corroded the adjacent metals.

Fig. 84. Front side of mother-of-pearl and cellulose-nitrate-composite belt buckle. Photo taken by Kelly L. Reddy-Best. Courtesy of URI Textile Conservation Collection.

Fig. 85. Back side of the mother-of-pearl and cellulose-nitrate-composite belt buckle in Fig. 84, showing crystals, which indicate decomposition of the cellulose nitrate. Photo taken by Kelly L. Reddy-Best. Courtesy of URI Textile Conservation Collection.

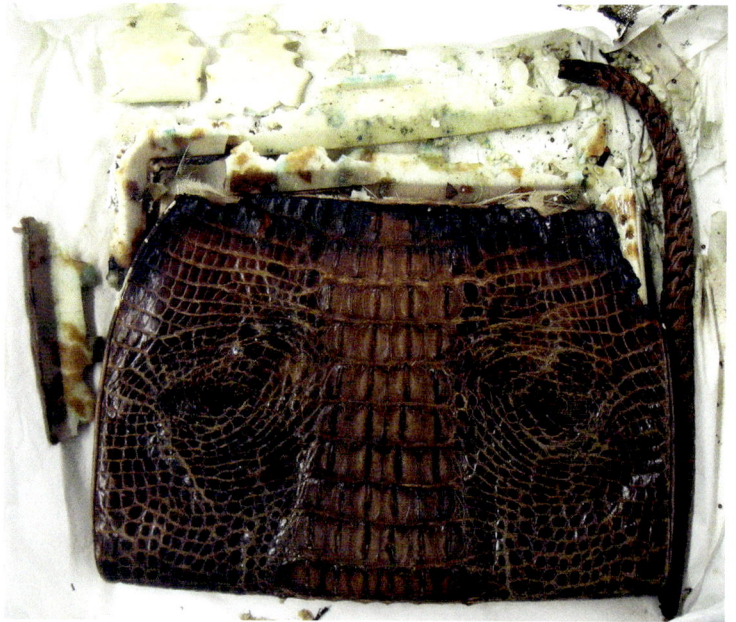

Fig. 86. Pre-1940 leather purse with metal clasp and cellulose-nitrate ornamentation that decomposed quickly once degradation was obvious. Photo taken by Kelly L. Reddy-Best. Courtesy of URI Textile Conservation Collection.

Fig. 87. Close-up of pre-1940 purse from Fig. 86, with metal clasp and cellulose-nitrate ornamentation. Blue-green and white salts indicate acid-corrosion of metal adjacent to cellulose-nitrate ornamentation. Photo taken by Kelly L. Reddy-Best. Courtesy of URI Textile Conservation Collection.

Recommendations for Cleaning, Storing, Handling, and Exhibiting Cellulose-Nitrate Accessories

- Do not clean degrading cellulose-nitrate objects that show crazing or porous areas.[14]
- Conduct a thorough search of the collection for cellulose-nitrate objects. Document each object with photographs to record its condition and then isolate the object, storing it in a glass or polypropylene (not cellulosic) container that allows for air circulation around the object.
- Monitor acidic emissions from a suspect cellulose-nitrate object by placing a low-pH indicator paper, such as a congo red strip, near the object while in isolation.

- Consider photographing and removing cellulose nitrate buttons, buckles, jewelry components, et cetera from garments and accessories before the degrading plastic damages the object to which it is attached.[15]
- If removal is not possible, place a barrier, such as polyethylene sheet or foam, between the accessory and the fabric.
- Store cellulose-nitrate objects in a dark, dry, well-ventilated area that is as cool as possible to delay decomposition.[16] Ideal relative humidity is 35–40 percent. Do not wrap or store in tightly closed containers or cabinets.[17]
- Routinely monitor objects for degradation. If decomposition progresses too far, the object is not salvageable; consider deaccessioning.
- Wear nitrile gloves when handling cellulose-nitrate objects if they are sweating plasticizer or acid and to protect handler's skin and avoid the potential of leaving fingerprints.[18]
- Do not allow steam to reach cellulose-nitrate components on fabrics if steaming is necessary to reduce wrinkles or creases.
- Access the condition of cellulose-nitrate components on or in all objects being considered for exhibition; humid and poorly ventilated conditions could accelerate degradation of cellulose-nitrate components as well as fabrics and metals.

Chronology of Cleaning, Exhibiting, and Storing Problems for Cellulose Nitrate

1862—By 1991, Parkesine objects had degraded, discolored, become embrittled, and shrunk.[19]

Post-1862—Report published in 1991 recorded that moisture had accelerated cellulose-nitrate degradation and the release of nitric acid.[20]

1920s—Cellulose-nitrate belt buckles decomposed over time (Figs. 83, 84, and 85).[21]

Pre-1940—Cellulose-nitrate ornamentation decomposed quickly once degradation began (Figs. 86 and 87).[22]

1940–50s—Nitrocellulose-plastic buttons decomposed over time, releasing nitric-acid gases.[23]

1947—Nitrocellulose-plastic buttons slowly released acid gases, damaging nearby fabrics (Fig. 88).[24]

1968—Nitrocellulose-plastic buttons changed color and decomposed over time, releasing nitric acid.[25]

Fig. 88. The nitrocellulose-plastic button on a vintage coat chemically decomposed and released nitric-acid fumes, which caused the hole. Courtesy of Drycleaning and Laundry Institute International (DLI) (*Clothes Care Gazette*, 1991).

Fig. 89. The components of an oval-shaped 1950s cellulose-acetate handbag that warped, wept, discolored, and off-gassed over time. Photo taken by Kelly L. Reddy-Best. Courtesy of URI Textile Conservation Collection.

Fig. 90. The metal hinge of the 1950s handbag in Fig. 89 has begun to corrode due to acid being released by cellulose acetate. Photo taken by Kelly L. Reddy-Best. Courtesy of URI Textile Conservation Collection.

(*Left*) Fig. 91. Cellulose-acetate bag. Photo taken by Margaret T. Ordoñez. Courtesy of URI Textile Conservation Collection.

(*Right*) Fig. 92. Side of cellulose-acetate bag from Fig. 91 that is warping. Photo taken by Susan Jerome. Courtesy of URI Textile Conservation Collection.

Cellulose-Acetate Accessories, Adornments, and Buttons

In 1926, cellulose acetate became the main thermoplastic molding material, and it remained so until polystyrene began replacing it after World War II. Low-molecular-weight plasticizers allowed cellulose acetate to be molded.[26] Manufacturers created buttons, sequins, beads, eyeglass frames, and accessories out of cellulose-acetate plastics from 1918 until 1978, if not longer.

Identification

Common degradation signs include distortion, shrinkage, stickiness, discoloration, embrittlement, delamination, fungal growth, and odors including an acidic, plastic, or, most commonly, a vinegar-like smell. The low-molecular-weight plasticizers migrate to the surface, causing distorting, shrinking, and weeping. They often formed blooms on the surface, especially when beads were in repeated contact with moisture. Plasticizer loss also leads to shrinkage.[27] Cellulose acetate tends to turn a blue-grey over time and cracks if exposed to sudden 3 to 4°F changes. Fig. 89 exhibits a 1950s handbag made of three different plastics: a clear, stable top and handles, a deforming cellulose-acetate body, and a very degraded detached unidentified plastic bottom with peeling and curling upper and lower layers (Fig. 90).[28] The body emits a strong vinegar-like smell and weeps when exposed to humidity. The acid has begun to attack the metal hinge.

Problems with Cleaning, Exhibiting, and Storing Cellulose-Acetate Accessories, Adornments, and Buttons

Although cellulose acetate naturally degrades over time, professional wet cleaning, dry cleaning, and steaming accelerated damage. Dry cleaning yellowed ornaments; professional wet cleaning dissolved

some early sequins; and steaming distorted, curled, and delustered cellulose-acetate plastics.

As cellulose acetate ages, it releases acetic-acid vapor, which can build up a storage container and accelerate decay of cellulose-acetate objects and adjacent components. Figs. 91 and 92 illustrate a cellulose-acetate handbag that is warping and weeping. Beads of acid solution collect on its surface even when isolated in a storage box.

Recommendations for Cleaning, Storing, Handling, and Exhibiting Cellulose-Acetate Accessories, Adornments, and Buttons

- Wipe objects with an absorbent dry cloth to remove dust or liquid that accumulates on the surface; do not wet with water or solvents.
- Conduct a thorough search of a collection for cellulose-acetate objects. Look for warping, off-gassing, and weeping. Photograph each object before degradation becomes too advanced to document its condition.
- Due to its inherent degradation, isolate an object in well-ventilated storage and closely monitor. A vinegar-like smell is one of the first warnings of decomposition.[29]
- Consider keeping degrading cellulose-acetate objects as teaching tools rather than deaccessioning them, if that is within the scope of the collection's mission.
- If removal is not possible, place a barrier of acid-free board, aluminum foil, or plastic film between the cellulose-acetate ornament and the fabric.
- Wear nitrile gloves when handling cellulose-acetate objects that have any liquid collecting on the surface.
- Do not steam cellulose-acetate ornaments.
- Access the condition of cellulose-acetate components on or in all objects being considered for exhibition; humid and poorly ventilated conditions could accelerate degradation of cellulose-acetate components as well as fabrics and metals.

Chronology of Cleaning and Exhibiting Problems for Cellulose-Acetate Accessories, Adornments, and Buttons

1950s—Cellulose-acetate handbag warped, wept, and discolored over time (Figs. 89 and 90).[30]

1966—Steaming distorted, curled, and delustered paillettes, or acetate discs, on designer dresses (Fig. 93).[31]

1978—Dry cleaning yellowed small, decorative cellulose-acetate discs.[32]

Fig. 93. Paco Rabanne's 1960s outer-space dresses. The paillette trim on the dresses curled and delustered during steaming. Courtesy of DLI (*Fabric Facts*, December 1966).

Polystyrene Buttons and Ornamentation

Polystyrene is a transparent molded plastic used in many buttons and garment adornments. First synthesized in 1830, it was not available on the commercial market until the mid-1930s.[33] Manufacturers frequently used inexpensive polystyrene to make flat, nondecorative plastic buttons that anchor coat buttons (Fig. 94) or secure inner tabs of waistbands.

Fig. 94. Clear polystyrene button on inside of 1960s coat. Photo taken by Margaret T. Ordoñez. Courtesy of URI HTCC, 2007.17.01.

Identification

Molded polystyrene objects are hard, rigid, and often clear and colorless—not a property of most other molded plastics. Polystyrene is soluble in acetone; test in an inconspicuous place.

Problems with Cleaning, Exhibiting, and Storing Polystyrene Buttons and Ornamentation

Polystyrene degraded over time, and objects cracked, crazed, or warped.[34] Exposure to light yellowed and increased brittleness of polystyrene.[35] Dry-cleaning solvents partially or completely dissolved polystyrene buttons and beads. Sometimes, partially dissolved buttons stained adjacent fabric. Paradichlorobenzene (mothballs) may have softened and damaged polystyrene objects.

Fig. 95. Polystyrene beads softened and partially dissolved in dry-cleaning solvent. Courtesy of DLI (*TABS*, 1984).

Recommendations for Cleaning, Storing, Handling, and Exhibiting Polystyrene Buttons and Ornamentation

- Do not dry clean garments with polystyrene buttons or beads attached. Figs. 95–97 show damage and distortion resulting from dry-cleaning solvent; acetone and petroleum spot removers also dissolve polystyrene.
- Use medium-temperature water and detergent to clean objects with polystyrene components, if needed.
- Identify and monitor polystyrene buttons and beads in a collection; these objects are slow to degrade but could have yellowed and embrittled; they will not emit harmful gases under normal storage conditions.
- Consider that polystyrene buttons or ornaments could be brittle when handling objects with these components.
- Do not steam polystyrene buttons or ornaments or let an iron get very close to buttons or ornaments if pressing a garment.
- Fasten polystyrene buttons with care; they may be brittle and crack with stress.

Fig. 96. Polystyrene beads on a sweater partially dissolved in dry-cleaning solvent and stained the adjacent fabric. Courtesy of DLI (*TABS*, 1990).

Chronology of Cleaning Problems for Polystyrene Buttons and Accessories

1940—Dry-cleaning solvent dissolved polystyrene buttons.[36]

1948—Steaming softened and partially dissolved polystyrene beads; the colors bled, staining adjacent fabrics.[37]

1953—Dry-cleaning solvent dissolved polystyrene buttons.[38]

1960s—Dry-cleaning solvent dissolved polystyrene buttons (Fig. 97).[39]

1969—Dry-cleaning solvent dissolved the polystyrene center of beads covered by a lacquerlike shell, leaving the bead distorted and flattened.[40]

1971—Dry cleaning softened and dissolved polystyrene buttons.[41]

1976—Dry-cleaning solvent partially or completely dissolved polystyrene beads.[42]

1984—Polystyrene beads softened and partially dissolved in dry-cleaning solvent (Fig. 95).[43]

1985—Dry-cleaning solvent dissolved polystyrene beads and buttons.[44]

1987—Dry-cleaning solvent dissolved and softened polystyrene buttons, which often transferred color to other portions of the garment.[45]

1987—Dry-cleaning solvent dissolved the center of round polystyrene beads covered by a lacquerlike shell, leaving the bead crushed and flattened.[46]

1989—Dry-cleaning solvent dissolved polystyrene plastics.[47]

1990—Dry-cleaning solvent dissolved polystyrene beads.[48]

1990—Dry cleaning dissolved, softened, and changed the shape of polystyrene beads and buttons.[49]

1990—Dry cleaning partially dissolved polystyrene beads and stained adjacent fabric (Fig. 96).[50]

1993—Dry-cleaning solvent dissolved beads on a sweater manufactured by The Limited.[51]

1995—Dry cleaning dissolved, cracked, and softened polystyrene ornamentation.[52]

Fig. 97. Close-up of a clear polystyrene button in Fig. 94 that partially dissolved in dry-cleaning solvent and adhered to the fabric surface. Photo taken by Susan Jerome. Courtesy of URI HTCC, 2007.17.01.

Garments with Polyurethane Foam

Commercial production of polyurethane foams began in the 1950s, and many fashion garments incorporated the soft, open-cell foam in the 1960s, continuing until the end of the century.[53] Manufacturers incorporated foams bonded to fabrics in garments for insulation and structural support to create a desired silhouette.

Fig. 98. Separated lining and fashion fabric with dark remnants on the white lining caused by the decomposition of the foam that once joined them, circa 1979. Photo taken by Susan Jerome. Courtesy of Linda Welter's Sample Textile Collection.

Identification

Twentieth-century polyurethane foam does not survive intact into the twentieth-first century. It stiffens, crumbles, or powders, retaining none of its original characteristics, and the garment or accessory that once had a crisp appearance and was flexible no longer retains that form (Fig. 98).

Problems with Cleaning, Exhibiting, and Storing Garments with Polyurethane Foam

Polyurethane foams naturally oxidized and deteriorated over time; their life expectancy was only three years. After three years, the foams yellowed, decomposed, crumbled, and produced a pungent odor. Some discolored and deteriorated in less than three years. Fine droplets of liquid could form on polyurethane foams.[54]

Oxidation was the primary cause of deterioration; moisture, light, and atmospheric-gas exposure accelerated damage.[55] Garments with polyurethane-foam components hanging in storage exhibited the greatest loss of foam in the shoulders, outer sides of sleeves, and the top of the collars and lapels due to light exposure. Garments that have been worn also exhibit damage in abraded areas, such as collar and cuff edges.[56]

Dry-cleaning and professional wet-cleaning treatments decomposed, darkened, stiffened, yellowed, crumbled, and discolored polyurethane foams. Dry cleaning shrank and blistered bonded foams and also separated bonded foams from their base fabric. As some foams decomposed, they became gummy and sticky.

Recommendations for Cleaning, Storing, Handling, and Exhibiting Garments with Polyurethane Foam

- Do not conservation wet clean or dry clean a garment containing polyurethane foam.
- Vacuum crumbled and powdered foam to prevent it from redepositing on the fabric and in the interstices between the yarns; preferably, the collection's vacuum cleaner has variable suction and a HEPA filter.
- Isolate all polyurethane foam objects in the collection.
- Limit light, air, and moisture exposure to delay deterioration; UV light particularly harms polyurethane. Decomposition is inevitable and irreversible and may cause harm to adjacent fabrics.
- Avoid bending, folding, or creasing stiffened foam; provide support for foam-lined, three-dimensional objects, as shown in Figs. 99 and 100, to help maintain their shape in storage and when on exhibition.

Chronology of Cleaning, Exhibiting, and Storing Problems for Garments with Polyurethane Foam

1960—Foam adhered to the backside of tricot lining in bathing suit hardened, crumbled, and partially peeled away from the lining, leaving it wrinkled and limp (Fig. 100).[57]

1960s—Foam in four foam-laminated dresses in a collection was off-gassing volatile organic acids that could damage neighboring materials and act in catalyzing further deterioration of the foam itself.[58]

1964—Dry cleaning decomposed some foam.[59]

1968—Polyurethane foam decomposed, yellowed, and stained adjacent fabric over time (Fig. 101).[60]

1969—Exposure to atmospheric gases and light oxidized and deteriorated urethane foams over time.[61]

1969—Dry cleaning caused foams to darken, stiffen, and decompose.[62]

1969—Foam between two knits decomposed and crumbled, leaving the fabrics separated (Fig. 98).[63]

1980—Many urethane foams yellowed, discolored, and crumbled away over time.[64]

1980—Light caused foams to darken, yellow, turn brown, and lose strength.[65]

1980—Some foams discolored and deteriorated in less than three years.[66]

1980—Foam products oxidized, darkened, and weakened over time.[67]

1989—Inexpensive foams yellowed and deteriorated permanently over time.[68]

Fig. 99. A circa 1960 Jantzen bathing suit with foam adhered to a tricot lining in the bosom area. Photo taken by Kelly L. Reddy-Best. Courtesy of URI Historic Textile and Costume Collection (HTCC), 2006.29.01.

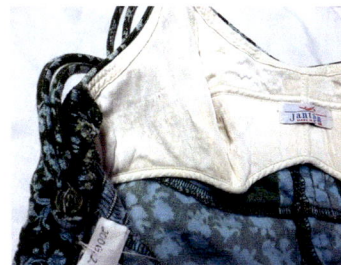

Fig. 100. Foam adhered to the backside of the tricot lining from the Jantzen bathing suit shown in Fig. 99 hardened, crumbled, and partially peeled away from the lining, leaving it wrinkled and limp. Photo taken by Susan Jerome. Courtesy of URI HTCC, 2006.29.01.

Fig. 101. Polyurethane foam (*left*) that yellowed over time and the stained upholstry fabric (*right*). Courtesy of DLI (*TABS*, 1968).

1989—Professional wet cleaning and dry cleaning caused inexpensive foams to become gummy and sticky.[69]

1991—Agitation during professional wet cleaning and dry cleaning caused foams to crumble and decompose.[70]

1991—Light yellowed polyurethane foams.[71]

1991—Dry cleaning accelerated damage and deterioration of foams.[72]

1991—Foams crumbled and stiffened from too much handling.[73]

1992—Foam naturally deteriorated over time.[74]

1997—Dry cleaning discolored foam shoulder-pad and cup materials.[75]

1997—Dry cleaning crumbled and decomposed some foams.[76]

Unspecified-Plastic Buttons, Beads, and Sequins Adornments

Many reports of problems did not specify the composition of problematic plastic objects, but the problems were numerous.

Identification

Conservation literature identifies physical clues, simple analysis, and analytical methods for material identification.[77] More important than determining the chemical composition of unidentified plastics is assessing their condition and making decisions on that basis.

Fig. 102. The unidentified-plastic beads' surfaces cracked and crazed during dry cleaning. Courtesy of DLI (*Fabric Facts*, 1969).

Problems with Cleaning, Exhibiting, and Storing Unspecified-Plastic Buttons, Beads, and Sequins Adornments

From 1940 to the end of the century, trade publications frequently reported plastic-adornment problems incurred during professional wet cleaning and dry cleaning. Heat applied during various professional wet cleaning processes yellowed, cracked, chipped, broke, and peeled the various embellishments. Dry cleaning caused similar problems—melting, deforming, and curling of plastics. Beads in Fig. 102 exhibited cracking and crazing resulting from dry cleaning, but this damage also could have occurred when the home launderer ironed a garment adorned with buttons like these. Both cleaning treatments caused some loss of the object's color.

Fig. 103. The beaded trim partially or completely dissolved during dry cleaning; the remaining beads stained the adjacent fabric. Courtesy of DLI (*Clothes Care Gazette*, 1996).

Dry cleaning garments with plastic adornments also damaged adjacent fabrics. As buttons dissolved, they often stuck to or stained other portions of the garment. Fig. 103 illustrates beads that softened and dissolved during dry cleaning and stained the adjacent fabrics.

Steam and age have decreased the stability of many twentieth-century plastic adornments. Steaming curled, faded, delustered, melted, softened, cracked, and deformed some unspecified-plastic adornments attached to garments. Fig. 104 illustrates color loss of button dyes, which stained the adjacent fabrics. Over time, unidentified-plastic adornments cracked, curled, and decomposed. Figs. 105 and 106 exhibit a handbag with ornaments that curled and discolored over time.

Recommendations for Cleaning, Storing, Handling, and Exhibiting Unspecified-Plastic Buttons, Beads, and Sequins Adornments

- Choose one ornament in as inconspicuous a place as possible if cleaning is absolutely necessary; apply water or detergent solution to the surface of the ornament with a slightly dampened cotton swab while observing changes to the surface. The high frequency of reported problems throughout the century makes testing plastic adornments with water before conservation wet cleaning imperative. If some of the ornaments have broken, test a small piece with the liquid in a clear glass container. Surface testing does not identify materials underneath coatings; interior plastics could be affected by water.
- Clean ornaments by wiping surfaces with a small dampened cotton swab after testing.
- Look for signs of deterioration in all plastic objects and ornaments; isolate a deteriorated object and store in a dark, cool, and dry area. Provide a ventilated container so that harmful emissions do not build up.
- Do not treat garments trimmed in nonremovable plastic ornamentation with paradichlorobenzene for an insect infestation. Thorough low-suction vacuuming and isolation or monitoring is the safer solution. Figs. 107 and 108 illustrate mothball damage and discoloration to unidentified-plastic sequins on a 1920s dress.
- Handle objects with sewn-on plastic ornaments carefully, in case degradation products have weakened the sewing threads or embrittled the plastic.
- Test all plastic adornments with steam in a subtle area before allowing steam to reach their surfaces; avoid hot steam—hold steam source at least 12 inches away from the object to provide cool moisture.
- Protect plastic ornaments, especially sequins and buttons, from steam when preparing a garment or accessory for exhibition.
- On exhibition, display in ventilated cases under low light levels. Distortion and degradation are inherent and irreversible with some plastic ornaments or objects.[78]

Fig. 104. The button dye bled onto the adjacent fabric during steaming. Courtesy of DLI (*TABS*, 1981).

Fig. 105. Purse with unspecified-plastic rectangular adornments that curled over time. Photo taken by Kelly L. Reddy-Best. Courtesy of URI Textile Conservation Collection.

Fig. 106. A close-up of the unspecified-plastic rectangular adornment in Fig. 105 that curled over time. Photo taken by Kelly L. Reddy-Best. Courtesy of URI Textile Conservation Collection.

Fig. 107. Unspecified-plastic sequins on a 1920s sequined and beaded dress deformed and discolored from contact with mothballs. The sequins could be polystyrene; paradicholorobenzene (mothballs) softens and damages polystyrene. Photo taken by Margaret T. Ordoñez. Courtesy of URI Textile Conservation Collection.

Fig. 108. Distorted sequins on the dress in Fig. 107. Photo taken by Susan Jerome. Courtesy of URI Textile Conservation Collection.

Chronology of Cleaning and Exhibiting Problems for Unspecified-Plastic Buttons, Beads, and Sequins Adornments

1920s—Unspecified-plastic rectangular adornments on a purse curled over time (Figs. 105 and 106).[79]

1920s—Unspecified-plastic sequins deformed and discolored from contact with paradichlorobenzene (mothballs) (Figs. 107 and 108).[80]

1937—Steaming curled and distorted sequins.[81]

1940—Steaming curled and distorted some sequins permanently.[82]

1944—Dry cleaning curled and distorted sequins and caused the sequins' colors to bleed.[83]

1945—Steaming caused some plastic buttons to bleed onto other portions of the garment.[84]

1948—Some translucent-plastic buttons grayed and lost color over time.[85]

1958—Steaming caused plastic buttons' dye to bleed onto adjacent fabrics.[86]

1958—Dry cleaning dissolved some plastic beads and caused stains on the adjacent fabric (Fig. 109).[87]

1958—Steaming distorted some sequins permanently (Fig. 109).[88]

1968—Dry cleaning and professional wet cleaning caused oxidized materials inside copper-coated porous beads to transfer and stain other portions of the garment.[89]

1969—Steaming caused some plastic buttons' dye to bleed onto adjacent fabrics.[90]

1969—Dry-cleaning solvent softened the black plastic core inside tiny metal-coated beads; the core deposited on and stained adjacent fabric.[91]

1969—Dry cleaning cracked and crazed some unidentified-plastic beads' surfaces (Fig. 102).[92]

1970s—Red sequins discolored during dry cleaning.[93]

1976—Steaming curled and delustered paillettes.[94]

1976—Some silver-coated plastic beads oxidized and turned black and sometimes stained adjacent fabric.[95]

1976—Steaming dulled, curled, and melted some plastic beads and sequins.[96]

1980s—Dry-cleaning solvent dissolved plastic acrylic button covers, and buttons stuck to portions of the garment.[97]

1980s—Dry-cleaning solvent dissolved sequins on wedding dresses.[98]

1981—Steaming caused dyes in buttons to bleed and stain adjacent fabric (Fig. 104).[99]

1984—Dry cleaning curled and discolored sequins.[100]

1985—Dry cleaning discolored sequins.[101]

1985—Steaming caused buttons to bleed and permanently stain adjacent fabrics.[102]

1985—Steaming curled and delustered some sequins.[103]

1986—Dry-cleaning solvent dissolved some dyes in plastic buttons.[104]

1987—Steaming damaged some sequins.[105]

1987—Many sequins lacked colorfastness during dry cleaning.[106]

1989—Dry-cleaning solvent dissolved and faded the colors of beads, and sequins adhered to wedding dresses.[107]

1989—Professional wet cleaning yellowed some plastic buttons.[108]

1989—Dry-cleaning solvent instantly dissolved sequins on an evening dress.[109]

1989—Dry cleaning cracked, chipped, and dissolved low-grade plastic buttons.[110]

1990—Professional wet cleaning and dry cleaning cracked, chipped, and broke plastic buttons.[111]

1990—Steaming dissolved button dyes, which stained adjacent fabrics.[112]

1991—Dry-cleaning solvent dissolved coloring matter in some sequins.[113]

1993—Dry cleaning and professional wet cleaning caused buttons to bleed, crack, chip, peel, and break.[114]

1993—Dry cleaning distorted and dissolved plasticlike objects with mirror effects.[115]

1995—Steaming curled and distorted some sequins.[116]

1996—Steaming caused buttons to bleed and stain adjacent fabrics.[117]

1996—Dry cleaning dissolved some beaded trims (Fig. 103).[118]

1998—Steam softened, cracked, and bent buttons.[119]

1998—Dry cleaning chipped, cracked, melted, discolored, and dissolved buttons.[120]

1998—Dry cleaning deformed, curled, and dissolved many sequins.[121]

1999—Dry-cleaning solvent dissolved and discolored fancy buttons.[122]

1999—Dry-cleaning solvent dissolved many sequins' dyes.[123]

1999—Steaming distorted some sequins.[124]

Fig. 109. Garment with three different sequin types. One bead type withstood dry cleaning; another (polystyrene) dissolved in dry-cleaning solvent, staining adjacent fabric; steaming distorted the third bead type (gelatin). Courtesy of DLI (Lyle, *Focus on Fabrics*, 451).

Appendix

Generic Manufactured Fiber and Yarn Trade Names and Dates

The following table lists manufactured fibers' and yarn brand names and dates referenced in publications consulted for this research. If a fiber brand name is known but not its generic fiber type, this lists provides the fiber as well as some of the dates that the brand was commercially available.

Fiber	Publication Date	Trade Name
Rayon—The Federal Trade Commission (FTC) designated *rayon* as the name for both regenerated cellulose and cellulose acetate.[1]	1924	
	1931	Bemberg, Celanese[2]
	1945	Bemberg, Celanese, Fiber D, Fiber G, Fortisan[3]
	1958	Avcoset, Avisco rayon, Bemberg, Briglo, Coloray, Colorspun rayon, Cordura, Covingtone—Dultone, Cupioni, DuPont rayon, Englo, Enka, Fibro, Fortisan, Fortisan 36, Hi-Narco, Ire, Jepspun, Matesa, Minifil, Mirco, Nub-Lite, Perlglo, Premier—Spun-lo, Suede Skin—Covinar, Rayflex, Skenandoa, Strongspun, Sunspun, Super-Narco, Tempra, Veri-Dul[4]
	1964	Abron, Avicolor, Avicron Avisco, Avril, Bemberg, Coloray, Corval, Cuprammonium, Fibro, Fortisan, Newbray, New-dull, Rayflex, Strawn, Super, Super Cordura, Super L, Topel, Viscose, Zantrel[5]

Fiber	Publication Date	Trade Name
	1970	Avicolor, Avicron, Avifil, Avisco, Avril, Avron, Bemberg, Celanese, Coloray, Cupioni, Cupracolor, Dy-Lok, Enka Rayon, Enkrome, Fiber H M, Fibro, Firemaker, Fortisan, Jetspun, Kolorbon, Lirelle, Matesa, Nupron, Parfe, Zantrel, Strawn, Xena[6]
	1972	Avril, Fortisan, Fortisan 36, Nupron, Xena, Zantrel[7]
	1975	Avril, Coloray, Enkrome, Zantrel[8]
	1976	Avicolor, Aviloc, Avril, Avril FR, Beau-Grip, Briglo, Coloray, Encel, Englo, Enka Enkrome, Fiber 40, Fiber 700, Fibro, Fibro DD, Fibro FR, FMC I.T., Jetspun, Kolorbon, SayFR, Skyloft, Softglo, Super White, Suprenka, Suprenka Hi Mod, Xena, Zantrel, Zantrell 700[9]
	1984	*HWM rayon:* Austria: Superfaser Belgium: Z 54 England: Vincel France: Z 54 Germany: Polyflox, Super Polyflox Italy: Koplon Switzerland: Z 54 Japan: Hipolan, Junlon, M 63, Polycot, Polyno, Tufcel USA: W 63, Zantrel[10]
	1999	*Rayon:* Beau-Grip, Fibro *HWM rayon:* Modal[11]
Acetate: FTC established separate categories for rayon and acetate.[12]	1953	
	1958	Avisco, Celanese, Celaperm, Celapow, Celaspun, Chromspun, Color-Sealed, Colorspun, DuPont, Estron, Quilpicel[13]
	1970	Acele, Avicolor, Avisco, Ceraloft, Celaperm, Chromspun, Estron, Loftura[14]
	1972	Celaperm, Chromspun[15]
	1975	Celara, Celaperm, Chromspun, Estron[16]
	1976	Acele, Ariloft, Avicolor, Celacloud, Celanese, Chromspun, Estron, Estron FMC, Loftura, SayFR, SLR[17]
	1999	Celanese, Celebrate, Chromspun, Estron, MicroSafe AM[18]

Fiber	Publication Date	Trade Name
Nylon	1958	Caprolan, Chemstrand, DuPont, IRC, Nylenka[19]
	1962	Caprolan[20]
	1964	Antron, Cadon, Caprolan, Cumuloft, Nyloft, Nylon by National, Nypel, Poliafil[21]
	1970	Antron, AstroTurf, Blue "C," Caprolan, Centrece, Cordura, Crepeset, Cumuloft, Dynel, Enka Nomex, Nylon, Nytelle, Qiana, Variline[22]
	1972	*nylon 6,6:* 501, Actionwear, Antron, Astroturf, Blue C by Monsanto, Cadon, Cumuloft, *nylon 6:* Ayrlyn, Caprolan, Celon, Crepeset, Enka, Grilon, Nytelle, Perlon, Touch[23]
	1975	Actionwear, Anso, Antron, Blue "C," Cadon, Cantrece, Caprolan, Captiva, Crepeset, Cumuloft, Enkaloft, Enkalure, Phillips 66, Qiana, Stryton[24]
	1976	Actionwear, Anso, Antron, Astroturf, Ayrlyn, Beaunit Nylon, Blue "C," Bodyfree, Cadon, Cantrece, Caprolan, Captiva, Cedilla, Celanese, Cordura, Courtlaulds Nylon, Crepeset, Cumuloft, Enka, Enkaloft, Enkalure, Enkalure II, Enkalure III, Enkasheer, Guaranteeth, Monvelle, Multisheer, Nylon BCF, Phillips 66, Phillips 66 Nylon, Qiana, Random-Set, Random Tone, Shareen, Source, Stria, Stryton, Super Bulk, Tango, Twix, Ultron, Variline, Zefran[25]
	1992	ACE, Anso, Antron series, Capima, Caplana, Caprolan, Caprolan Sea Gard, Captiva, Crème de Captiva, Cordura, Crepeset, DriSilque, FREEDOM, Hydrofil, Jentell, Lexes, Matinesse, Microsupplex, No-Shock, Patina, Resistat, Shimmereen, Silky Touch, Stay Gard, Supplex, Tactel, Traffic Control Fiber System, Trilene, Trimax, Tru-Ballistic, Ultron, Ultron 3D, Wear Dated, Wear Dated II, Wellon, Wellstrand, Zefsport, Zeftron 200, Zetron fiber series[26]
	1999	Anso IV, Antron, Caprolan, Captiva, Hydrofil, Supplex, Tactel[27]
Casein-based fibers	1939–1948	Aralac[28]
	1940s–1965	Fibrolane (Britain)[29]
	1937–1940s	Lanitol (Italy)[30]
	1940s–late 60s	Merinova (Italy)

Fiber	Publication Date	Trade Name
Saran	1958	Saran, Velon[31]
	1964	Lus-Trus, Rovana, Saran by National, Velon[32]
	1970	Lus-Trus, Rovana, Vectra[33]
	1975	Lus-Trus[34]
	1977	Rovana, Saran[35]
	1999	Saran[36]
Modacrylic	1962	Dynel, Verel[37]
	1964	Aeress, Dynel, Verel[38]
	1970	Verel[39]
	1972	Dynel, Excelon, Kanekalon, Teklan, Verel[40]
	1975	Dynel, SEF, Verel[41]
	1976	A-Acrilan, Acrilan, Elura, Orlon, Sef, Verel[42]
	1999	SEF[43]
Acrylic	1956	Acrilan, Dynel, Orlon, X-51[44]
	1958	Acrilan, Creslan, Dynel, Orlon, Verel[45]
	1962	Acrilan, Creslan, Courtelle, Dynel, Orlon, Verel, Zefran [46]
	1964	Acrilan, Acrilan-Spectran, Creslan, Oron, Orlon-Sayelle, Zefkrome, Zefran[47]
	1969	Acrilan, Creslan, Orlon, Zefran[48]
	1970	Acrilan, Creslan, Orlon, Zefran II[49]
	1972	18 types of Acrilan, Anywear, Bi-Loft, 11 types of Creslan, Nomel, 16 types of Orlon, Glace, Sayelle, Wintuk, Zefkrome[50]
	1975	Dynel, SEF, Verel[51]
	1976	A-Acrilan, Acrilan, Elura, Orlon, Sef, Verel[52]
	1992	Acrilan, Bi-loft, Bulkaire, CFFR, CPF, Creslan, CTF, CYLIGHT, Duraspun, Fi-Lana II, MicroSupreme, Pil-Trol, Sayelle, Sno-Brite, So-Lara, Wintuk[53]

Fiber	Publication Date	Trade Name
Polyester	1962	Dacron, Fortrel, Kodel, Teron, Vycron[54]
	1964	Dacron, Fortrel, Kodel, Vycron[55]
	1970	Avlin, Blue "C," Dacron, Encron, Fortrel, Kodel, Quintess, Vycron[56]
	1972	Amilar, Blue C, Dacron, Diolen, Encron, Fiber V, Fortrel, Kodel, Terital, Tergal, Teriber, Terlenka, Teron, Terylene, Tetoron, Toray, Tough-Stuff, Trevira, Vycron Crimplene[57]
	1975	Avlin, Dacron, Encron, Fortrel, Golden Touch, Kodel, Quintess, Spectran, Strialine, Trevira[58]
	1976	Avlin, Blue "C," Dacron, Encron, Encron 8, Encron MCS, Enka, Esterweld, Fiber 200, Fortrel, Fortrel 7, Golden Touch, Guaranteeth, Kodel, Quintess, Source, Spectran, Strialine, Textura, Trevira, Vycron, Zefran[59]
	1977	Dacron, Fortrel, Kodel[60]
	1982	A-Tell, Dacron, Kodel[61]
	1999	ACE Series, Comfortrel, Compet, Dacron, DSP, ESP, FiberBrite 2000, Fitwell, Fortrel, Fortrel EcoSpun, Gard, Hollofil, Micrell, Micromatique, NatureTex Pentron, Polarguard, Polystrand, Pro Earth, Stay Coolmax, Softec Dacron, Tairilin, Thermax, Thermostat, Trevira, Trevira II, Universe, Wellene[62]
Spandex	1958	Fiber K[63]
	1964	Lycra, Vyrene[64]
	1969	Lycra[65]
	1970	Blue "C," Lycra, Numa, Vyrene[66]
	1972	Duraspan, Estane V.C., Fulflex, Glospan, Interspan, Numa, Unel[67]
	1975	Lycra[68]
	1976	Lycra, Monvelle[69]
	1977	Lycra, Spandelle, Vyrene[70]
	1992	Cheerspan, Glospan, Lycra[71]
	1999	Dorlastan, Glospan, Lycra[72]

Notes

Introduction

1. American Institution of Conservation, "Environmental Guidelines," *Wiki: A Collaborative Knowledge Resource,* May 12, 2020, https://www.conservation-wiki.com/wiki/Environmental_Guidelines.

2. King, *Textile Identification, Conservation, and Preservation,* 51.

3. American Institution of Conservation, "Environmental Guidelines."

4. For a survey form, see "What Is the Condition of the Collection," *POPART: Preservation Of Plastic AR-Tifacts in museum collections,* http://popart-highlights.mnhn.fr/collection-survey/what-is-the-condition-of-the-collection/index.html.

5. See University of Alaska Museum of the North, "Deaccessioning and Disposal," https://www.uaf.edu/museum/collections/ethno/policies/deaccessioning/. Museums & Galleries NSW, an Australian organization, offers guidelines on deaccessioning and disposal in small museums. See Museums & Galleries NSW, "Deaccession and Disposal in Small Museums," *Sustaining Places,* Sept. 2012, https://sustainingplaces.files.wordpress.com/2012/09/deaccession-and-disposal-in-small-museums.pdf. The Society of American Archivists provides a more thorough discussion of reappraisal and deaccessioning. See Reappraisal and Deaccessioning Development and Review Team, revised by the Technical Subcommittee on Guidelines for Reappraisal and Deaccessioning, "Guidelines for Reappraisal and Deaccessioning [2017]," Society of American Archivists website, revised May 2017, https://www2.archivists.org/sites/all/files/GuidelinesForReappraisalDeaccessioning_2017.pdf. The Association of Art Museum Directors provides guidance on the purpose and process of deaccessioning and disposal. See "AAMD Policy on Deaccessioning," Association of Art Museum Directors website, amended Oct. 2015, https://aamd.org/sites/default/files/document/AAMD%20Policy%20on%20Deaccessioning%20website_0.pdf. The American Alliance of Museums also outlines ethics, guidelines, and recommendations for deaccessioning objects, and it offers a useful rubric to guide decision making. See American Alliance of Museums, "Direct Care of Collections: Ethics, Guidelines, and Recommendations," American Alliance of Museums website, updated Mar. 2019, https://www.aam-us.org/programs/ethics-standards-and-professional-practices/direct-care-of-collections/.

6. Collier, Bide, and Tortora, *Understanding Textiles,* 54.

7. Timar-Balazsky and Eastop, *Chemical Principles of Textile Conservation,* 126.

8. Collier, Bide, and Tortora, *Understanding Textiles,* 440.

9. Collier, Bide, and Tortora, *Understanding Textiles,* 25.

10. Collier, Bide, and Tortora, *Understanding Textiles,* 542.

11. Wingate, *Fairchild's Dictionary of Textiles* (1979), 4.

12. Collier, Bide, and Tortora, *Understanding Textiles,* 542.

13. Collier, Bide, and Tortora, *Understanding Textiles,* 543.

14. Collier, Bide, and Tortora, *Understanding Textiles,* 9.

15. Collier, Bide, and Tortora, *Understanding Textiles,* 47.

16. Timar-Balazsky and Eastop, *Chemical Principles of Textile Conservation,* 323.

17. Collier, Bide, and Tortora, *Understanding Textiles,* 46.

18. Collier, Bide, and Tortora, *Understanding Textiles,* 23.

19. Judy Logan, "Care and Cleaning of Iron." *CCI Notes* 9/6, Canadian Conservation Institute, 2007, https://www.canada.ca/en/conservation-institute/services/conservation-preservation-publications/canadian-conservation-institute-notes/care-iron.html.

1. Fibers

1. Collier, Bide, and Tortora, *Understanding Textiles,* 4, 114–15; Lyle, *Modern Textiles,* 23–24.

2. Denny's 1923 book of definitions has an entry titled "Artificial Silk" and includes nitrocellulose and cuprammonium from cotton linters and a "newer" viscose process that used wood pulp. Denny, *Fabrics and How to Know Them,* 17.

3. A committee appointed by the National Retail Dry Goods Association of the United States chose the "distinctive name" *rayon.* Woolman and McGowan, *Textiles,* 206.

4. Tortora, *Understanding Textiles,* 93.

5. Cohen and Johnson, *J. J. Pizzuto's Fabric Science,* 49; Collier, Bide, and Tortora, *Understanding Textiles,* 127–29.

6. Editors of American Fabrics and Fashions Magazine, *Encyclopedia of Textiles,* 9, 12. US production of cuprammonium rayon ceased in 1975, but other countries continued making the fiber and marketing its products worldwide. Tortora, *Understanding Textiles,* 91.

7. Collier, Bide, and Tortora, *Understanding Textiles,* 127–29.

8. For longitudinal and cross-sectional microscopic views of rayon, see Muhammad Rehan Ashraf, "Structure of Viscose Rayon," *Textile Insight,* Sept. 14, 2014, https://textileinsight.blogspot.com/2014/09/structure-of-viscose-rayon.html.

9. National Institute of Drycleaning (NID), *Fabric Facts* (June 1964).

10. Dewey, "Pure Textile," 227.

11. Rath, "Artificial Silk," 426.

12. National Association of Dyers and Cleaners (NADC), *Bulletin Service* (Dec. 1940).

13. NADC, *Bulletin Service* (Dec. 1940).

14. Dress in the Textile Conservation Collection University of Rhode Island (URI), Kingston, RI.

15. Heard, "Wartime Developments in Textiles and Clothing," 430.

16. Heard, "Wartime Developments in Textiles and Clothing," 222.

17. NADC, *Bulletin Service* (Feb. 1948).

18. NADC, *Bulletin Service* (Nov. 1949).

19. Lyle, *Focus on Fabrics,* 260.

20. NID, *Fabric Facts* (Apr. 1960).

21. NID, *Fabric Facts* (June 1964).

22. International Fabricare Institute (IFI), *Fabrics and Fashions* (1987).

23. IFI, *Fabrics and Fashions* (Jan. 1988).

24. IFI, *Clothes Care Gazette* (Feb. 1990).

25. Price, Cohen, and Johnson, *J. J. Pizzuto's Fabric Science,* 55.

26. IFI, *Fabrics and Fashions* (May 1996).

27. Storms, "Paper Textiles," 452.

28. Correspondence between Margaret T. Ordoñez and Martha W. Grimm, Oct. 4, 2021. Martha Grimm treated paper dresses for an exhibition at the Phoenix Art Museum. With permission from Helen Jean, Jacquie Dorrance Curator of Fashion, she shared information about the dresses and her conservation treatments.

29. Label on child's paper dress: "Waste Basket Boutique, by Mars of Ashville, NC," Phoenix Art Museum, L109.202.

30. Storms, "Paper Textiles," 452.

31. Storms, "Paper Textiles," 452.

32. Storms, "Paper Textiles," 452.

33. Jonathan Walford, "Paper Dresses," Vintage Fashion Guild website, 2008, https://vintagefashionguild.org/fashion-history/paper-dresses/.

34. Merle B. Shaw and George W. Bicking, "Rayon as a Paper-Making Material," *Journal of Research* 4, no. 2 (1929): 203, 210–11.

35. Paper shirt, 1960s, ISU TCM, C107.

36. Correspondence between Margaret T. Ordoñez and Martha W. Grimm, Sept. 5, 2021.

37. Child's paper dress, 1960s, ISU TCM, 2010.412.

38. Collier, Bide, and Tortora, *Understanding Textiles,* 138, 143, 145; Hollen and Saddler, *Textiles,* 58.

39. For a longitudinal view of acetate, see "1970–1979, Yves Saint Laurent, Red, Black and White Silk Organza Dress, Acetate Lining," *Conservation and Art Materials Encyclopedia Online (CAMEO),* Museum of Fine Arts, Boston, Aug. 22, 2017, http://cameo.mfa.org/wiki/1970-1979,_Yves_Saint_Laurent,_red,_black_and_white_silk_organza_dress,_acetate_lining.

40. Lyle, *Focus on Fabrics,* 384, 387.

41. NADC, *Technical Bulletin* (Sept. 1932).

42. NADC, *Technical Bulletin* (Jan. 1933).

43. Evans and McGowan, *Guide to Textiles,* 57.

44. Blue-purple acetate fabric sample that fume faded, Sample in URI Textile Science Collection.

45. Lyle, *Focus on Fabrics,* 260.

46. Lyle, *Focus on Fabrics,* 28.

47. Acetate and nylon skirt, URI Historic and Textile Costume Collection (HTCC), 1979.08.06.

48. Cowan and Jungerman, *Introduction to Textiles,* 76.

49. NID, *Fabric Facts* (June 1964).

50. NID, *Fabric Facts* (June 1964).

51. NID, *Fabric Facts* (Dec. 1973).

52. IFI, *TABS* (1975).

53. IFI, *TABS* (1975).

54. Lyle, *Modern Textiles,* 71.

55. IFI, *Fabrics and Fashions* (Nov. 1981).

56. Kerr, "Potential Problems When Drycleaning Twentieth Century Garments," 75.

57. IFI, *Clothes Care Gazette* (1990).

58. IFI, *TABS* (Mar. 1994).

59. Hollen and Saddler, *Textiles,* 58.

60. Collier and Tortora, *Understanding Textiles,* 151.

61. IFI, *Clothes Care Gazette* (Jan. 1997).

62. Collier, Bide, and Tortora, *Understanding Textiles,* 47.

63. Collier, Bide, and Tortora, *Understanding Textiles,* 212.

64. NADC, *Bulletin Service* (Dec. 1946).

65. Hollen and Saddler, *Textiles,* 78.

66. Lyle, *Focus on Fabrics,* 36.

67. Lyle, *Focus on Fabrics,* 36.

68. NID, *Fabric Facts* (Feb. 1965).

69. Price, Cohen, and Johnson, *Fabric Science,* 57.

70. Price, Cohen, and Johnson, *Fabric Science,* 57.

71. Collier, Bide, and Tortora, *Understanding Textiles,* 153.

72. For a photomicrograph and information on nylon, see "Du Pont Nylon," *CAMEO,* May 13, 2020, http://cameo.mfa.org/wiki/Du_Pont_Nylon.

73. Kornreich, *Introduction to Fibers and Fabrics,* 18.

74. Hollen and Saddler, *Textiles,* 62.

75. Hollen and Saddler, *Textiles,* 62.

76. Lyle, *Focus on Fabrics,* 34.

77. Hollen and Saddler, *Textiles,* 72.

78. Joseph, *Introductory Textile Science,* 126.

79. Manufacturers marketed peanut-based protein fibers as Ardil in Britain from 1951 to 1957 ("Ardil," *CAMEO,* Apr. 29, 2016, http://cameo.mfa.org/wiki/Ardil) and fibers from corn (zein) protein as Vicara in the United States from 1948 to 1957 ("Zein Fiber," *CAMEO,* May 30, 2020, http://cameo.mfa.org/wiki/Zein_fiber; Tortora, *Understanding Textiles,* 132). These azlon products did not have the same problems as casein-based fabrics.

80. Woolman and McGowan, *Textiles,* 239.

81. Woolman and McGowan, *Textiles,* 243; "Aralac. You've Heard about It . . . You've Seen It . . . You've Worn It . . . but What Is It?" *Life* magazine, May 22, 1944, 94, cited in Katie Rodger, "Back to the Future? Milk Fibers in the 21st Century," *Splash! Milk Science Update,* Mar. 2019, https://milkgenomics.org/article/back-to-the-future-milk-fibers-in-the-21st-century/.

82. Woolman and McGowan, *Textiles,* 243; Tortora, *Understanding Textiles,* 132.

83. Tortora, *Understanding Textiles,* 132.

84. "Azlon Fiber," *CAMEO,* Dec. 5, 2020, http://cameo.mfa.org/wiki/Azlon_fiber.

85. Collier, Bide, and Tortora, *Understanding Textiles,* 218.

86. NADC, *Bulletin Service* (1946).

87. NADC, *Bulletin Service* (1946).

88. Wingate, *Textile Fabrics and Their Selection* (1970), 411.

89. IFI, *Fabrics and Fashions* (Sept. 1991); for more information on polyester, see "Polyester Fiber," *CAMEO,* Oct. 21, 2020, http://cameo.mfa.org/wiki/Polyester_fiber.

90. For a photomicrograph of polyester (both dull and bright fibers), see "McFadden, Aqua Polyester Pleated Dress," *CAMEO,* Aug. 22, 2017, http://cameo.mfa.org/wiki/1970-1979,_McFadden,_aqua_polyester_pleated_dress.

91. NID, *Fabric Facts* (Oct. 1961).

92. Hollen and Saddler, *Textiles,* 79.

93. Lyle, *Modern Textiles,* 175.

94. Collier, Bide, and Tortora, *Understanding Textiles,* 542, 176, 180.

95. Steele, *Fifty Years of Fashion,* 68–69.

96. For microscopic view of acrylic filaments, see "FRIL: Acrylic," *CAMEO,* Aug. 22, 2017, http://cameo.mfa.org/wiki/Category:FRIL:_Acrylic; also search *CAMEO* for brand names.

97. Collier, Bide, and Tortora, *Understanding Textiles,* 179.

98. NID, *Fabric Facts* (Aug. 1953).

99. NID, *Technical Bulletin Service* (June 1953).

100. NID, *Fabric Facts* (Aug. 1953).

101. Lyle, *Focus on Fabrics,* 38.

102. NID, *Fabric Facts* (June 1963).

103. IFI, *Fabrics and Fashions* (July 1980).

104. IFI, *Fabrics and Fashions* (Sept. 1991).

105. IFI, *Fabrics and Fashions* (Sept. 1991).

106. Collier, Bide, and Tortora, *Understanding Textiles,* 184.

107. "Modacrylic Fiber," *CAMEO,* Dec. 5, 2020, http://cameo.mfa.org/wiki/Modacrylic_fiber.

108. Kadolph and Langford, *Textiles,* 123.

109. NID, *Fabric Facts* (Oct. 1953).

110. NID, *Fabric Facts* (Oct. 1953).

111. Hollen and Saddler, *Textiles,* 75.

112. Collier, Bide, and Tortora, *Understanding Textiles,* 204; "Rubber Fiber," *CAMEO,* May 30, 2020, http://cameo.mfa.org/wiki/Rubber_fiber.

113. Collier, Bide, and Tortora, *Understanding Textiles,* 204; Cohen and Johnson, *Fabric Science,* 57.

114. NID, *Fabric Facts* (Oct. 1955).

115. Lyle, *Focus on Fabrics,* 487.

116. Lyle, *Focus on Fabrics,* 510.

117. NID, *TABS* (1969).

118. Men's pants, ca. 1970, URI HTCC, 2002.12.01.

119. Prichard and Smith, "Taking a Risk: Collecting for the Future," 134.

120. Lyle, *Focus on Fabrics,* 147.

121. Lyle, *Modern Textiles,* 195.

122. IFI, *TABS* (1982).

123. IFI, *Fabrics and Fashions* (Jan. 1983).

124. IFI, *Fabrics and Fashions* (1983).

125. Kerr, "Potential Problems When Drycleaning Twentieth Century Garments," 75.

126. Grattan, "Problem of Rubber Conservation," 125.

127. IFI, *Clothes Care Gazette* (Oct. 1989).

128. IFI, *TABS* (1989).

129. IFI, *Clothes Care Gazette* (Feb. 1989).

130. IFI, *Clothes Care Gazette* (Oct. 1989).

131. IFI, *TABS* (1989).

132. IFI, *Clothes Care Gazette* (July 1990).

133. IFI, *Clothes Care Gazette* (Dec. 1992).

134. IFI, *Clothes Care Gazette* (Mar. 1993).

135. For specific brands, see "Spandex," *Encyclopedia of Fashion,* Advameg, http://www.fashionencyclopedia.com/fashion_costume_culture/ModernWorld-1980-2003/Spandex.html.

136. "Spandex Fiber," *CAMEO,* Dec. 4, 2020, http://cameo.mfa.org/wiki/Spandex_fiber.

137. Stout, *Introduction to Textiles,* 216.

138. Hollen and Saddler, *Textiles,* 92.

139. Miss Hawaii bathing suit, 1970s, URI HTCC, 1994.07.18.

140. Lyle, *Focus on Fabrics,* 78.

141. Smith and Block, *Textiles in Perspective,* 150.

142. IFI, *TABS* (1982).

143. Collier and Tortora, *Understanding Textiles,* 197.

144. Price, Cohen, and Johnson, *Fabric Science,* 56.

2. Fabric Constructions

1. National Institute of Drycleaning (NID), *Fabric Facts* (Apr. 1971).
2. International Fabricare Institute (IFI), *Fabrics and Fashions* (Sept. 1981).
3. Denny, *Fabrics and How to Know Them*, 46.
4. Collier, Bide, and Tortora, *Understanding Textiles*, 184.
5. National Institute of Cleaning and Dyeing, *Fabric Facts* (Feb. 1951).
6. NID, *Practical Operation Tips* (Apr. 1971).
7. IFI, *TABS* (1973).
8. IFI, *Fabric & Fashions* (Nov. 1980).
9. IFI, *Fabric & Fashions* (Nov. 1988).
10. IFI, *Fabric & Fashions* (Nov. 1988).
11. IFI, *Clothes Care Gazette* (Mar. 1988).
12. IFI, *Clothes Care Gazette* (Oct. 1990).
13. Cohen and Johnson, *J. J. Pizzuto's Fabric Science*, 191; Collier, Bide, and Tortora, *Understanding Textiles*, 443.
14. National Association of Dyers and Cleaners (NADC), *Bulletin Service* (Feb. 1938).
15. NADC, *Bulletin Service* (Feb. 1938).
16. NID, *Technical Bulletin Service* (Apr. 1954).
17. NID, *TABS* (1969).
18. Imitation-suede boot, ca. 1970s, Iowa State University Textiles and Museum, 9981828.a.b.
19. IFI, *Fabric Facts* (Nov. 1972).
20. IFI, *Fabric Facts* (Nov. 1972).
21. Patricia Helms, interviewed by Kelly L. Reddy-Best, Jan. 22, 2010, Kingston, RI.
22. IFI, *TABS* (1984).
23. IFI, *Clothes Care Gazette* (Feb. 1988).
24. IFI, *TABS* (1992).

3. Printed Components

1. Collier, Bide, and Tortora, *Understanding Textiles*, 424; Lyle, *Focus on Fabrics*, 115.
2. Collier, Bide, and Tortora, *Understanding Textiles*, 424; Lyle, *Focus on Fabrics*, 119–20.
3. Kadolph and Langford, *Textiles*, 318
4. Lyle, *Focus on Fabrics*, 120.
5. National Institute of Drycleaning, *Fabric Facts* (June 1958).
6. International Fabricare Institute (IFI), *Fabric Facts* (Apr. 1972).
7. IFI, *Laundry Analysis Bulletin Service* (1976).
8. IFI, *Laundry Analysis Bulletin Service* (1982).
9. IFI, *Clothes Care Gazette* (Mar. 1990).
10. IFI, *Clothes Care Gazette* (Mar. 1990).
11. IFI, *Clothes Care Gazette* (May 1993).
12. Lyle, *Focus on Fabrics*, 115.
13. Wingate, *Fairchild's Dictionary of Textiles* (1967), 327.
14. Editors of American Fabrics and Fashions Magazine, *Encyclopedia of Textiles*, 559.
15. National Association of Dyers and Cleaners (NADC), *Bulletin Service* (July 1950).
16. Lyle, *Focus on Fabrics*, 115.

17. Lyle, *Focus on Fabrics*, 442.
18. IFI, *Fabrics and Fashions* (Mar. 1974).
19. Lyle, *Focus on Fabrics*, 286.
20. IFI, *Clothes Care Gazette* (Feb. 1989).

4. Coatings

1. Wingate, *Fairchild's Dictionary of Textiles* (1979), 136.
2. International Fabricare Institute (IFI), *Clothes Care Gazette* (Mar. 1995, Jan. 1988).
3. IFI, *TABS* (1976).
4. IFI, *Clothes Care Gazette* (Jan. 1988).
5. IFI, *Clothes Care Gazette* (Mar. 1995).
6. IFI, *Clothes Care Gazette* (Mar. 1995).
7. Wingate, *Fairchild's Dictionary of Textiles* (1979), 199.
8. IFI, *Clothes Care Gazette* (Jan. 1997).
9. IFI, *Fabrics and Fashions* (Nov. 1985).
10. IFI, *Clothes Care Gazette* (Feb. 1995).
11. IFI, *TABS* (July 1996).
12. IFI, *Clothes Care Gazette* (Jan. 1997).
13. Kerr and Batcheller, "Degradation of Polyurethanes," 190, 192.
14. Kerr and Batcheller, "Degradation of Polyurethanes," 193–97.
15. Kerr and Batcheller, "Degradation of Polyurethanes," 194.
16. Quye and Williamson, *Plastics: Collecting and Conserving*, 117.
17. National Institute of Drycleaning (NID), *Fabric Facts* (Dec. 1971).
18. IFI, *Fabrics and Fashions* (Nov. 1973).
19. IFI, *TABS* (1975).
20. IFI, *TABS* (1977).
21. IFI, *Fabrics and Fashions* (Sept. 1980).
22. IFI, *TABS* (1980).
23. IFI, *TABS* (1982).
24. IFI, *Fabrics and Fashions* (Mar. 1983).
25. IFI, *Fabrics and Fashions* (1985).
26. IFI, *Fabrics and Fashions* (1987).
27. IFI, *Fabrics and Fashions* (1987).
28. IFI, *Clothes Care Gazette* (Mar. 1988).
29. IFI, *Fabrics and Fashions* (Sept. 1990).
30. IFI, *Clothes Care Gazette* (1990).
31. IFI, *Fabrics and Fashions* (Sept. 1994).
32. Collier, Bide, and Tortora, *Understanding Textiles*, 379.
33. Quye and Williamson, *Plastics*, 111–21, 127–28.
34. Quye and Williamson, *Plastics*, 111–21, 127–28.
35. Quye and Williamson, *Plastics*, 109–10.
36. Shashoua, "Conservation of Plastics," 14.
37. Shashoua, "Conservation of Plastics," 15.
38. National Association of Dyers and Cleaners (NADC), *Bulletin Service* (Feb. 1946).
39. NADC, *Bulletin Service* (Feb. 1946).
40. NADC, *Bulletin Service* (Feb. 1946).
41. NADC, *Bulletin Service* (Feb. 1946).
42. NADC, *Bulletin Service* (Aug. 1947).
43. NID, *Fabric Facts* (Dec. 1963).

44. IFI, *TABS* (1973).

45. IFI, *Textile Cleaning Technology* (1973).

46. IFI, *Textile Cleaning Technology* (1973).

47. Lyle, *Modern Textiles,* 215.

48. Prichard and Smith, "Taking a Risk," 135.

49. IFI, *Technical Bulletin Service* (Mar. 1982).

50. IFI, *Clothes Care Gazette* (Feb. 1988).

51. IFI, *Clothes Care Gazette* (June 1989).

52. Coated fabric samples in the University of Rhode Island Textile Science Collection.

53. Prichard and Smith, "Taking a Risk," 134–35.

54. Denny, *Fabrics and How to Know Them,* 83.

55. Advertisement for OMO dress shields, *Leavenworth (KS) Times,* May 16, 1896, newspapers.com/clip/12155134/omo-dress-shields/.

56. NID, *Fabric Facts* (Aug. 1959).

57. Lyle, *Focus on Fabrics,* 155.

58. Lyle, *Focus on Fabrics,* 155.

59. IFI, *Fabric Facts* (Aug. 1959).

60. Rita Hindle, interviewed by Kelly L. Reddy-Best, Jan. 15, 2010, Kingston, RI.

61. Hindle interview.

62. IFI, *TABS* (1978).

63. IFI, *Fabrics and Fashions* (Sept. 1978).

64. IFI, *Fabrics and Fashions* (Sept. 1978).

65. IFI, *Clothes Care Gazette* (Oct. 1987).

66. IFI, *Clothes Care Gazette* (Oct. 1989).

67. IFI, *Fabrics and Fashions* (Mar. 1994).

68. IFI, *Fabrics and Fashions* (Mar. 1994).

69. IFI, *Fabrics and Fashions* (Mar. 1994).

5. Adhesives

1. National Association of Dyers and Cleaners (NADC), *Bulletin Service* (May 1939).

2. NADC, *Bulletin Service* (Dec. 1940).

3. Lyle, "Challenge of Textile Problems," 86.

4. National Institute of Drycleaning (NID), *Fabric Facts* (Feb. 1968).

5. Arnold Scassi dress, University of Rhode Island Historic Textile and Costume Collection, 1997.01.24.

6. International Fabricare Institute (IFI), *Fabrics and Fashion* (1985).

7. Evenson and Crews, "Effects of Light and Ageing," 34.

8. IFI, *Clothes Care Gazette* (Sept. 1987).

9. IFI, *Clothes Care Gazette* (Sept. 1988).

10. IFI, *TABS* (1988).

11. Evenson and Crews, "Effects of Light and Ageing," 34.

12. IFI, *Clothes Care Gazette* (June 1990).

13. IFI, *Clothes Care Gazette* (Sept. 1993).

14. IFI, *Clothes Care Gazette* (Feb. 1995).

15. IFI, *Clothes Care Gazette* (Jan. 1996).

16. Collier, Bide, and Tortora, *Understanding Textiles,* 375–77.

17. Fuleihan and Morris, "Maintenance Methods for a Fabric-Foam Laminate," 39.

18. NID, *TABS* (1967).

19. NID, *TABS* (1967).

20. IFI, *TABS* (1968).

21. Patricia Helms, interviewed by Kelly L. Reddy-Best, Jan. 22, 2010, Kingston, RI.

22. Helms interview.

23. IFI *Fabrics Fashions Bulletin* (Sept. 1980).

24. IFI, *Technical Bulletin Service* (July 1978).

25. IFI, *TABS* (1985).

26. IFI, *Fabrics and Fashions* (May 1991).

27. IFI, *TABS* (1991).

28. IFI, *Fabrics and Fashions* (Nov. 1992).

29. Kerr and Batcheller, "Degradation of Polyurethanes," 189.

30. Lyle, *Modern Textiles,* 321.

31. Lyle, *Modern Textiles,* 321; Wingate, *Fairchild's Dictionary of Textiles* (1979), 309.

32. See Qian Zhang and Chi-Wai Kan, "Review of Fusible Interlinings Usage in Garment Manufacture," table 1.

33. NID, *Fabrics Facts* (Feb. 1962).

34. Drycleaning and Laundry Institute International, *TABS* (1968).

35. Helms interview.

36. IFI, *TABS* (1973).

37. IFI, *LABS* (1977).

38. IFI, *LABS* (1988).

39. IFI, *LABS* (1983).

40. IFI, *LABS* (1983).

41. Drycleaning and Laundry Institute International, *TABS* (1985).

42. IFI, *Clothes Care Gazette* (May 1988).

43. IFI, *TABS* (1991).

44. IFI, *TABS* (1991).

45. IFI, *Fabrics and Fashions* (1993).

46. IFI, *TABS* (1994).

47. IFI, *Clothes Care Gazette* (Mar. 1995).

48. IFI, *Clothes Care Gazette* (June 1995).

49. IFI, *TABS* (1995).

50. IFI, *TABS* (1995).

51. IFI, *TABS* (Sept. 1998).

52. NID, *Fabric Facts* (June 1965). The trademark expired in 1985: see "CHEM STITCH: Trademark Details," *Justia Trademarks,* https://trademarks.justia.com/721/75/chem-stitch-72175112.html.

53. NID, *Fabric Facts* (June 1965).

54. NID, *Fabric Facts* (Apr. 1968).

55. Sample in Margaret T. Ordoñez's Sample Textile Collection.

56. Woolman and McGowan, *Textiles,* 256–57.

57. IFI, *Clothes Care Gazette* (Nov. 1992).

58. NID, *Fabric Facts* (June 1961).

59. NADC, *Bulletin Service* (June 1946).

60. NADC, *Bulletin Service* (Dec. 1949).

61. NADC, *Fabric Facts* (Apr. 1950).

62. Lyle, *Focus on Fabrics,* 159.

63. NID, *Fabric Facts* (June 1961).

64. NID, *Fabric Facts* (June 1961).

65. NID, *Fabric Facts* (June 1961).

66. NID, *Fabric Facts* (June 1961).

67. NID, *Fabric Facts* (Apr. 1963).

68. NID, *Fabric Facts* (Oct. 1971).

69. IFI, *TABS* (1973).

70. IFI, *Technical Bulletin Service* (July 1975).

71. Lyle, *Modern Textiles,* 217.

72. Lyle, *Modern Textiles,* 217.

73. Lyle, *Modern Textiles,* 218.

74. IFI, *Fabrics and Fashions* (Nov. 1988).

75. IFI, *Clothes Care Gazette* (Oct. 1992).

76. IFI, *Clothes Care Gazette* (Nov. 1992).

77. IFI, *TABS* (May 1995).

78. IFI, *TABS* (Nov. 1999).

79. IFI, *Clothes Care Gazette* (1958).

80. Lyle, *Focus on Fabrics,* 514.

81. IFI, *Clothes Care Gazette* (Dec. 1988).

82. IFI, *Clothes Care Gazette* (Nov. 1993).

83. NICD, *Technical Bulletin Service* (May 1951).

84. NICD, *Fabric Facts* (Aug. 1951).

85. Hollen and Saddler, *Textiles,* 146.

86. NID, *Fabric Facts* (Feb. 1957).

87. Lyle, *Focus on Fabrics,* 380.

88. IFI, *Clothes Care Gazette* (Jan. 1995).

89. IFI, *Fabrics & Fashions* (Mar. 1996).

6. Finishes

1. Lyle, *Focus on Fabrics,* 323.

2. Lyle, *Focus on Fabrics,* 324.

3. International Fabricare Institute (IFI), *Fabrics and Fashions* (July 1975).

4. IFI, *Clothes Care Gazette* (Oct. 1989).

5. IFI, *Fabric Facts* (Oct. 1990).

6. Denny, *Fabrics and How to Know Them,* 28.

7. Editors of *American Fabrics and Fashions* Magazine, *Encyclopedia of Textiles,* 529.

8. Jacobson and O'Brien, "Discoloration of Cotton Fabrics," 59.

9. National Association of Dyers and Cleaners (NADC), *Bulletin Service* (1935).

10. NADC, *Bulletin Service* (1936).

11. IFI, *Fabrics and Fashions* (1974).

12. Collier, Bide, and Tortora, *Understanding Textiles,* 441–42

13. Tortora and Merkel, *Fairchild's Dictionary of Textiles,* 365.

14. NADC, *Bulletin Service* (Apr. 1938).

15. National Institute of Drycleaning (NID), *Fabric Facts* (June 1955).

16. Lyle, *Focus on Fabrics,* 443.

17. Lyle, *Focus on Fabrics,* 286.

18. Kornreich, *Introduction to Fibers and Fabrics,* 167.

19. IFI, *Fabrics and Fashions* (1987).

20. IFI, *Clothes Care Gazette* (Feb. 1989).

21. IFI, *Clothes Care Gazette* (May 1990).

22. Collier, Bide, and Tortora, *Understanding Textiles,* 278, 395, 482.

23. IFI, *TABS* (1988).

24. Jacobson and O'Brien, "Discoloration of Cotton Fabrics," 61.

25. Denny, *Fabrics and How to Know Them,* 63.

26. NICD, *Bulletin Service* (Mar. 1950).

27. NICD, *Fabric Facts* (June 1952).

28. NID, *Fabric Facts* (Dec. 1956).

29. NID, *Fabric Facts* (Dec. 1956).

30. Lyle, *Focus on Fabrics,* 303.

31. IFI, *Fabrics and Fashions* (Apr. 1989).

32. IFI, *TABS* (1988).

33. IFI, *Clothes Care Gazette* (Nov. 1984).

34. IFI, *Fabrics and Fashions* (July 1990).

35. Collier, Bide, and Tortora, *Understanding Textiles,* 452–53.

36. Editors of *American Fabrics and Fashions* Magazine, *Encyclopedia of Textiles,* 411.

37. Wingate, *Fairchild's Dictionary of Textiles* (1967), 200.

38. IFI, *Fabrics and Fashions* (July 1990); Hall, *Textile Finishing,* 342–45.

39. Collier, Bide, and Tortora, *Understanding Textiles,* 454.

40. Stout, Zillgitt, and Ferraro, "Effects of Laundering and Drycleaning," 199.

41. Stout, Zillgitt, and Ferraro, "Effects of Laundering and Drycleaning," 199.

42. Cowan, *Introduction to Textiles,* 247.

43. Cowan and Jungerman, *Introduction to Textiles,* 196.

44. Hull, "Housewives' Opinions," 775.

45. NID, *Fabric Facts* (Feb. 1964).

46. NID, *Fabric Facts* (Apr. 1965).

47. NID, *Fabric Facts* (Apr. 1965).

48. Harper and Treece, "Permanent Press in Fabrics," 666.

49. Patricia Helms, interviewed by Kelly L. Reddy-Best, Jan. 22, 2010, Kingston, RI.

50. IFI, *TABS* (May 1980).

51. IFI, *TABS* (1988).

52. IFI, *TABS* (1988).

53. IFI, *Fabrics and Fashions* (July 1995).

54. Collier and Tortora, *Understanding Textiles,* 388.

55. Collier, Bide, and Tortora, *Understanding Textiles,* 458–60; Denny, *Fabrics and How to Know Them,* 105–6.

56. NID, *Technical Bulletin Service* (Sept. 1953).

57. Lyle, *Modern Textiles,* 250.

7. Plastics

1. Quye and Williamson, *Plastics,* 11–14, 18.

2. Waheed ul-Hassan, "Polyurethanes History," *Polyurethanes—Foam, Manufacturing Process, Raw Materials, Suppliers,* Feb. 17, 2008, urethanestechnology.blogspot.com/2008/02/polyurethanes-history.html.

3. Quye and Williamson, *Plastics,* 17–19, 22.

4. Wiles, "Changes in Polymeric Materials," 105–12; Bechthold, "Wet Look in 1960s Furniture Design," 128–32; George Prytulak, "Display and Storage of Museum Objects Containing Cellulose Nitrate," *CCI Notes* 15/3, Canadian Conservation Institute, 1998, https://www.canada.ca/en/conservation-institute/services/conservation-preservation-publications/canadian-conservation-institute-notes/display-storage-objects-cellulose-nitrate.html; Reilly, "Celluloid Objects," 145–62; Fenn, "Plastic Beads and Buttons," 53–63; Quye, "Historical Plastics Come of Age," 617–20; Blank, "Introduction to Plastics and Rubbers," 53–63.

5. Madden and Learner, "Preserving Plastics," 5. For a brief overview of plactics' degradation, see van Oosten, "Preserving Plastic," 137–38. An international research effort from 2008 to 2012 identified methods to analyze plastics, investigated their degradation, and provided practical guidance for conservation and care of plastic cultural heritage objects. This Preservation Of Plastic ARTefacts in Museum Collections (POPART) project published a book of its findings (Lavédrine, Founier, and Martin, *Preservation of Plastic Artefacts*) and held a conference; some of the presentations are at the POPART website: http://popart-highlights.mnhn.fr/.

6. Coughlin and Seeger, "You Collected What?!," 120.

7. Quye and Williamson, *Plastics*, 11–13; Hillman, "Short History of Early Consumer Plastics," 20–22.

8. Robert Friedel discusses "celluloid's role as imitating finer and more expensive materials" and includes pictures of celluloid picture frames, a decorative comb, and the comb, brush, hand mirror, and boxes in a toilet (vanity) set. Friedel, "Is It Real?" 51.

9. Reuss, "Whodunnit?" 114. Reuss sumised that a number of unlabeled cellulose-nitrate objects in the Linden Museum in Stuttgart, Germany, could have been made in specialized factories in Gablonz, Czechoslovakia, "which may be seen as the imitator of the world's adornment." These bead exports had worldwide distribution in the beginning of the twentieth century.

10. Carey, "Potential Hazards in Caring for Ethnographic Beadwork," 110. For information about a test for cellulose nitrate, see R. Scott Williams, "The Diphenylamine Spot Test for Cellulose Nitrate in Museum Objects," *CCI Notes* 17/2, 1994, Canadian Conservation Institute, https://www.canada.ca/en/conservation-institute/services/conservation-preservation-publications/canadian-conservation-institute-notes/diphenylamine-test-cellulose-nitrate.html. Note: a sample of the suspect material must be taken for the test.

11. Quye and Williamson, *Plastics*, 134; Coles, "Challenge of Materials?" 127.

12. Quye and Williamson, *Plastics*, 113–14, 121; Coughlin and Seeger, "You Collected What?" 121.

13. Fenn, "Plastic Beads and Buttons," 56, 132–34.

14. Morgan, "Joint Project on the Conservation of Plastics," 49.

15. Carey, "Potential Hazards." Carey reports that the British Museum's Department of Ethnography dismantled a Somali necklace to separate disintegrating cellulose nitrate beads that were causing blue-green copper nitrate crystals to form on the silver components and white crystals on Venetian glass beads.

16. Quye and Williamson, *Plastics*, 87; Mossman, "Plastic in the Science Museum, London," 31.

17. Coles, "Challenge of Materials?" 129.

18. Mossman, "Plastic in the Science Museum, London," 31.

19. Mossman, "Plastic in the Science Museum, London," 30.

20. Morgan, "Joint Project on the Conservation of Plastics," 49.

21. Belt buckles in the University of Rhode Island (URI) Textile Conservation Collection.

22. Purse in the URI Textile Conservation Collection.

23. Patricia Helms, interviewed by Kelly L. Reddy-Best, Jan. 22, 2010, Kingston, RI.

24. National Institute of Cleaning and Dyeing, *Bulletin Service* (Jan. 1947).

25. National Institute of Drycleaning (NID), *TABS* (1968).

26. Quye and Williamson, *Plastics*, 13–14; Fenn, "Plastic Beads and Buttons," 59.

27. Mossman and Abel, "Testing Treatments to Slow Down the Degradation of Cellulose Acetate," 106–7.

28. Wilcox, *Century of Bags*, 72; Fenn, "Plastic Beads and Buttons," 59; Crow, "Stop the Rot," 44.

29. Crow, "Stop the Rot," 44; Quye and Williamson, *Plastics*, 87.

30. Handbag in the URI Textile Conservation Collection.

31. NID, *Fabric Facts* (1966).

32. International Fabricare Institute (IFI), *Fabrics and Fashions* (Mar. 1978).

33. Quye and Williamson, *Plastics*, 17–18.

34. Quye and Williamson, *Plastics*, 113, 118, 121.

35. Fenn, "Plastic Beads and Buttons," 61.

36. National Institute of Cleaning and Dyeing (NADC), *Bulletin Service* (Oct. 1940).

37. Lyle, "Button! Button!," 192.

38. NID, *Technical Bulletin Service* (May 1953).

39. Coat with polystyrene buttons in the URI Historic Textile and Costume Collection (HTCC), 2007.17.01.

40. NID, *Clothes Care Gazette* (1969).

41. NID, *TABS* (1971).

42. Lyle, *Modern Textiles*, 325.

43. IFI, *TABS* (1984).

44. IFI, *Fabrics and Fashions* (1985).

45. IFI, *Fabrics and Fashions* (July 1987).

46. IFI, *Fabrics and Fashions* (July 1987).

47. IFI, *Fabrics and Fashions* (July 1989).

48. IFI, *Clothes Care Gazette* (June 1990).

49. IFI, *TABS* (1990).

50. IFI, *TABS* (1990).

51. IFI, *Not in Vogue* (Jan. 1993).

52. IFI, *Clothes Care Gazette* (Feb. 1995).

53. Kerr and Batcheller, "Degration of Polyurethanes," 189.

54. IFI, *Fabrics and Fashions* (1980); Quye and Williamson, *Plastics*, 119, 130.

55. Quye and Williamson, *Plastics*, 131–32.

56. Kerr and Batcheller, "Degradation of Polyurethanes," 197.

57. Jantzen bathing suit in the URI HTCC, 2006.29.01.

58. Garside and Lovett, "Polyurethane Foam," 77.

59. Labarthe, *Textiles*, 347.

60. NID, *TABS* (1968).

61. NID, *Practical Operating Tips* (1969).

62. NID, *TABS* (1969).

63. Sample fabric of fashion fabric that was once joined to a foam backing, in Linda Welter's Sample Textile Collection.

64. IFI, *Fabrics and Fashions* (Sept. 1980).

65. IFI, *Fabrics and Fashions* (Sept. 1980).

66. IFI, *Fabrics and Fashions* (1980).

67. IFI, *Fabrics and Fashions* (Sept. 1980).

68. IFI, *Fabrics and Fashions* (Mar. 1989).

69. IFI, *Fabrics and Fashions* (Mar. 1989).

70. IFI, *Clothes Care Gazette* (June 1991).

71. Kerr and Batcheller, "Degradation of Polyurethanes," 194.

72. Kerr and Batcheller, "Degradation of Polyurethanes," 197.

73. Kerr and Batcheller, "Degradation of Polyurethanes," 203.

74. IFI, *Fabrics and Fashions* (Nov. 1992).

75. IFI, *Fabrics and Fashions* (May 1997).

76. IFI, *Fabrics and Fashions* (May 1997).

77. Quye and Williamson, *Plastics,* 54–83; Reilly, "Celluloid Objects," 156–57; Blank, "Introduction to Plastics and Rubbers," 55–56; Katz, *Early Plastics,* 29–30.

78. Quye and Williamson, *Plastics,* 87, 137.

79. Sample in URI Textile Conservation Collection.

80. Sample in URI Textile Conservation Collection.

81. NADC, *Bulletin Service* (Oct. 1937).

82. NADC, *Bulletin Service* (Dec. 1940).

83. NADC, *Bulletin Service* (Dec. 1944).

84. NADC, *Bulletin Service* (June 1945).

85. Lyle, "Button! Button!," 192.

86. Lyle, *Focus on Fabrics,* 447.

87. Lyle, *Focus on Fabrics,* 451.

88. Lyle, *Focus on Fabrics,* 451.

89. NID, *Fabric Facts* (Dec. 1968).

90. NID, *TABS* (1969).

91. NID, *TABS* (Feb. 1969).

92. NID, *Fabric Facts* (1969).

93. NID, *Fabrics and Fashions* (2005).

94. Lyle, *Modern Textiles,* 326.

95. Lyle, *Modern Textiles,* 326.

96. Lyle, *Modern Textiles,* 326.

97. Helms interview.

98. Helms interview.

99. IFI, *TABS* (1981).

100. IFI, *TABS* (1984).

101. IFI, *Fabrics and Fashions* (1985).

102. IFI, *Fabrics and Fashions* (1985).

103. IFI, *Fabrics and Fashions* (1985).

104. IFI, *TABS* (1986).

105. IFI, *TABS* (1987).

106. IFI, *Fabrics and Fashions* (May 1987).

107. IFI, *Fabrics and Fashions* (July 1987).

108. IFI, *Fabrics and Fashions* (July 1989).

109. IFI, *Clothes Care Gazette* (Jan. 1989).

110. IFI, *TABS* (1989).

111. IFI, *Clothes Care Gazette* (May 1990).

112. IFI, *Clothes Care Gazette* (Aug. 1990).

113. IFI, *TABS* (1991).

114. IFI, *Clothes Care Gazette* (Jan. 1993).

115. NID, *Fabric Facts* (Dec. 1966).

116. NID, *Fabric Facts* (Sept. 1995).

117. NID, *Fabric Facts* (Apr. 1996).

118. NID, *Clothes Care Gazette* (1996).

119. IFI, *TABS* (May 1998).

120. IFI, *TABS* (May 1998).

121. IFI, *Frabrics and Fashions* (Jan. 1998).

122. IFI, *Industry Focus* (Jan. 1999).

123. IFI, *TABS* (July 1999).

124. IFI, *TABS* (July 1999).

Appendix

1. Collier, Bide, and Tortora, *Understanding Textiles,* 139.

2. Paddock, *Textile Fibers and Their Use,* 232.

3. Potter, *Fiber to Fabric,* 232.

4. Lyle, *Focus on Fabrics,* 26.

5. Labarthe, *Textiles: Origins to Usage,* 260–61.

6. Wingate, *Textile Fabrics and Their Selection* (1970), 47–49.

7. Joseph, *Introductory Textile Science,* 70, 72.

8. Wingate, Gillespie, and Milgrom, *Know Your Merchandise,* 117.

9. Lyle, *Modern Textiles,* 363.

10. Cook, *Handbook of Textile Fibres: Man-Made Fibres,* 52.

11. Price, Cohen, and Johnson, *Fabric Science,* 55.

12. Collier, Bide, and Tortora, *Understanding Textiles,* 139.

13. Lyle, *Focus on Fabrics,* 30.

14. Wingate, *Textile Fabrics and Their Selection* (1970), 42.

15. Joseph, *Introductory Textile Science,* 86.

16. Wingate, Gillespie, and Milgrom, *Know Your Merchandise,* 117.

17. Lyle, *Modern Textiles,* 363.

18. Price, Cohen, and Ingrid, *Fabric Science,* 52.

19. Lyle, *Focus on Fabrics,* 34.

20. Stout, *Introduction to Textiles,* 177.

21. Labarthe, *Textiles,* 299.

22. Wingate, *Textile Fabrics and Their Selection* (1970), 44–45.

23. Joseph, *Introductory Textile Science,* 119.

24. Wingate, Gillespie, and Milgrom, *Know Your Merchandise,* 117.

25. Lyle, *Modern Textiles,* 367.

26. Collier and Tortora, *Understanding Textiles,* 158–59.

27. Price, Cohen, and Johnson, *Fabric Science,* 54.

28. Tortora, *Understanding Textiles,* 132.

29. Tortora, *Understanding Textiles,* 132.

30. Tortora, *Understanding Textiles,* 132.

31. Lyle, *Focus on Fabrics,* 47–49.

32. Labarthe, *Textiles,* 333.

33. Wingate, *Textile Fabrics and Their Selection* (1970), 50.

34. Wingate, Gillespie, and Milgrom, *Know Your Merchandise,* 117.

35. Alexander, *Textile Products,* 11.

36. Price, Cohen, and Johnson, *Fabric Science,* 61.

37. Stout, *Introduction to Textiles,* 198.

38. Labarthe, *Textiles,* 303.

39. Wingate, *Textile Fabrics and Their Selection* (1970), 44.

40. Joseph, *Introductory Textile Science,* 150.

41. Wingate, Gillespie, and Milgrom, *Know Your Merchandise,* 117.

42. Lyle, *Modern Textiles,* 364.

43. Price, Cohen, and Johnson, *Fabric Science,* 59.

44. Hollen and Saddler, *Textiles,* 66.

45. Lyle, *Focus on Fabrics,* 37–43.

46. Cowan, *Introduction to Textiles,* 111; Stout, *Introduction to Textiles,* 186.

47. Labarthe, *Textiles,* 302–3.

48. Cowan and Jungerman, *Introduction to Textiles,* 88.

49. Wingate, *Textile Fabrics and Their Selection* (1970), 42–43.

50. Joseph, *Introductory Textile Science,* 144.

51. Wingate, Gillespie, and Milgrom, *Know Your Merchandise,* 117.

52. Lyle, *Modern Textiles,* 364.

53. Tortora and Collier, *Understanding Textiles,* 180.

54. Stout, *Introduction to Textiles,* 203.

55. Labarthe, *Textiles,* 317.

56. Wingate, *Textile Fabrics and Their Selection* (1970), 46.

57. Joseph, *Introductory Textile Science,* 128–29.

58. Wingate, Gillespie, and Milgrom, *Know Your Merchandise,* 117.

59. Lyle, *Modern Textiles,* 369.

60. Alexander, *Textile Products,* 11.

61. Smith and Block, *Textiles in Perspectives,* 131.

62. Tortora and Collier, *Understanding Textiles,* 171.

63. Cowan and Jungerman, *Introduction to Textiles,* 97.

64. Labarthe, *Textiles,* 342.

65. Cowan and Jungerman, *Introduction to Textiles,* 97.

66. Wingate, *Textile Fabrics and Their Selection* (1967), 50.

67. Joseph, *Introductory Textile Science,* 171.

68. Wingate, Gillespie, and Milgrom, *Know Your Merchandise,* 117.

69. Lyle, *Modern Textiles,* 370–71.

70. Alexander, *Textile Products,* 11.

71. Collier and Tortora, *Understanding Textiles,* 200.

72. Price, Cohen, and Johnson, *Fabric Science,* 56.

Bibliography

Alexander, Patsy. *Textile Products: Selection, Use, and Care.* Boston: Houghton Mifflin, 1977.

American Alliance of Museums. "Direct Care of Collections: Ethics, Guidelines, and Recommendations." American Alliance of Museums website. Updated Mar. 2019. https://www.aam-us.org/programs/ethics-standards-and-professional-practices/direct-care-of-collections/.

American Institution of Conservation. "Environmental Guidelines." *Wiki: A Collaborative Knowledge Resource.* https://www.conservation-wiki.com/wiki/Environmental_Guidelines.

"Aralac. You've Heard about It . . . You've Seen It . . . You've Worn It . . . but What Is It?" *Life* magazine, May 22, 1944, 94.

Ashraf, Muhammad Rehan. "Structure of Viscose Rayon." *Textile Insight.* Sept. 14, 2014. https://textileinsight.blogspot.com/2014/09/structure-of-viscose-rayon.html.

Association of Art Museum Directors. "AAMD Policy on Deaccessioning." Association of Art Museum Directors website. Amended Oct. 2015. https://aamd.org/sites/default/files/document/AAMD%20Policy%20on%20Deaccessioning%20website_0.pdf.

"Aralac. You've Heard about It . . . You've Seen It . . . You've Worn It . . . but What Is It?" *Life* magazine, May 22, 1944, 94.

Bechthold, Tim. "Wet Look in 1960s Furniture Design: Degradation of Polyurethane-Coated Textile Carrier Substrates." In Rogerson and Garside, *Future of the 20th Century,* 128–33.

Blank, Sharon. "An Introduction to Plastics and Rubbers in Collections." *Studies in Conservation* 35 (1990): 53–63.

Carey, Margaret. "Potential Hazards in Caring for Ethnographic Beadwork." In Wright, *Ethnographic Beadwork,* 103–12.

"CHEM STITCH: Trademark Details." *Justia Trademarks.* https://trademarks.justia.com/721/75/chem-stitch-72175112.html.

Cohen, Allen, and Ingrid Johnson. *J. J. Pizzuto's Fabric Science.* New York: Fairchild Books, 2010.

Coles, Fran. "Challenge of Materials? A New Approach to Collecting Modern Materials at the Science Museum, London." In Keneghan and Egan, *Plastics,* 125–31.

Collier, Billie, Martin Bide, and Phyllis Tortora. *Understanding Textiles.* 7th ed. Upper Saddle River, NJ: Pearson Prentice Hall, 2009.

Collier, Billie, and Phyllis Tortora. *Understanding Textiles.* 5th ed. Upper Saddle River, NJ: Prentice-Hall, 1997.

Conservation and Art Materials Encyclopedia Online (CAMEO). Museum of Fine Arts, Boston. http://cameo.mfa.org/.

Cook, Gordon. *Handbook of Textile Fibres: Man-Made Fibres.* Durham, UK: Merrow, 1984.

Coughlin, Mary, and Ann M. Seeger. "You Collected What?! The Risks and Rewards of Acquiring Cellulose Nitrate." In Keneghan and Egan, *Plastics,* 119–24.

Cowan, Mary, and Martha Jungerman. *Introduction to Textiles.* 2nd ed. New York: Meredith, 1969.

Cowan, Mary. *Introduction to Textiles.* New York: Appleton-Century-Crofts, 1962.

Crow, James. "Stop the Rot." *New Scientist* 42 (June 19, 2010): 42–45.

Denny, Grace Goldena. *Fabrics and How to Know Them: Definitions of Fabrics Practice, Textiles Tests, Classification of Fabrics.* Philadelphia: J. B. Lippincott, 1923.

Dewey, L. H. "Pure Textile." *Journal of Home Economics* 6, no. 3 (June 1914): 222–28.

Editors of American Fabrics and Fashions Magazine. *Encyclopedia of Textiles.* Englewood Cliffs, NJ: Prentice-Hall, 1980.

Encyclopedia of Fashion. Advameg. http://www.fashion encyclopedia.com/.

Evenson, Janet, and Patricia Cox Crews. "The Effects of Light and Ageing on Selected Quilting Products Containing Adhesives." *Journal of the American Institute for Conservation* 44, no. 1 (2005): 27–38.

Evans, Mary, and Ellen McGowan. *A Guide to Textiles.* New York: John Wiley & Sons, 1939.

Fenn, Julia. "Plastic Beads and Buttons in Social History Collections: A Dilemma." In Wright *Ethnographic Beadwork,* 56–63.

Fuleihan, Mary Ann, and Mary Ann Morris. "Maintenance Methods for a Fabric-Foam Laminate." *Journal of Home Economics* 58, no. 1 (Jan. 1966): 36–40.

Friedel, Robert. "Is It Real? Imitation and Originality in Plastics." In Madden, Charola, Cobb, DePriest, and Koestler, *Age of Plastic,* 51–60.

Garside, Paul, and Doon Lovett. "Polyurethane Foam: Investigating the Physical and Chemical Consequences of Degradation." In Rogerson and Garside, *Future of the 20th Century,* 77–83.

Grattan, David. "The Problem of Rubber Conservation." In Grattan, *Saving the Twentieth Century,* 125–28.

———, ed. *Saving the Twentieth Century: The Conservation of Modern Materials.* Ottawa: Communications Canada, 1993.

Hall, A. J. *Textile Finishing.* London: Heywood Books, 1957.

Harper, Patricia Beverly, and Anna Jean Treece. "Permanent Press in Fabrics for Home Sewing." *Journal of Home Economics* 59, no. 8 (Oct. 1967): 664–66.

Heard, Earl. "Wartime Developments in Textiles and Clothing." *Journal of Home Economics* 34, no. 7 (Sept. 1942): 427–32.

Hillman, David. "A Short History of Early Consumer Plastics." *Journal of the Canadian Association for Conservation* 10 and 11 (1985–86): 20–27.

Hollen, Norma, and Jane Saddler. *Textiles.* New York: Macmillan, 1964.

Hull, David. "Housewives' Opinions of and Experiences with Easy Care, Wash-Wear Clothing." *Journal of Home Economics* 55, no. 10 (Dec. 1963): 773–76.

Jacobson, Lydia, and Ruth O'Brien. "The Discoloration of Cotton Fabrics in Laundering." *Journal of Home Economics* 15, no. 2 (Feb. 1923): 59–63.

Joseph, Marjory. *Introductory Textile Science.* 2nd ed. New York: Holt, Rinehart & Winston, 1972.

Joseph, Marjory, and Audrey G. Gieseking, *Illustrated Guide to Textiles.* 2nd ed. Fullerton, CA: Plycon Press, 1972. (Swatches are from a custom set prepared for the Textiles and Clothing Department, University of Tennessee, Knoxville, 1973.)

Kadolph, Sarah, and Anna L. Langford. *Textiles.* 8th ed. Upper Saddle River, NJ: Prentice Hall, 1998.

Katz, Sylvia. *Early Plastics.* 2nd ed. Buckinghamshire, UK: Shire, 1999.

Keneghan, Brenda, and Louise Egan. *Plastics: Looking at the Future and Learning from the Past.* London: Archetype, 2008.

Kerr, Nancy. "Potential Problems When Drycleaning Twentieth Century Garments." In *20th Century Materials, Testing and Textile Conservation: 9th Symposium,* edited by Harpers Ferry Regional Textile Group Symposium, 75–76. Washington, DC: Harpers Ferry Region Textile Group, 1998.

Kerr, Nancy, and Jane Batcheller. "Degradation of Polyurethanes in Twentieth-Century Museum Textiles." In Grattan, *Saving the Twentieth Century,* 189–206.

King, Rosalie Rosso. *Textile Identification, Conservation, and Preservation.* Park Ridge, NJ: Noyes Publications, 1985.

Kornreich, Ernest. *Introduction to Fibers and Fabrics: Their Manufacture and Properties.* London: American Elsevier, 1966.

Labarthe, Jules. *Textiles: Origins to Usage.* New York: Macmillan, 1964.

Lavédrine, Bertrand, Alban Fournier, and Graham Martin. *Preservation of Plastic Artefacts in Museum Collections.* [Paris]: Comité des Travaux Historiques et Scientifiques, 2012.

Logan, Judy. "Care and Cleaning of Iron." *CCI Notes* 9/6. Canadian Conservation Institute. 2007. https://www.canada.ca/en/conservation-institute/services/conservation-preservation-publications/canadian-conservation-institute-notes/care-iron.html.

Lyle, Dorothy. "Button! Button! What's Wrong with the Buttons." *Journal of Home Economics* 40, no. 4 (Apr. 1948): 191–92.

———. "The Challenge of Textile Problems." *Journal of Home Economics* 43, no. 2 (Feb. 1951): 85–88.

———. *Focus on Fabrics.* Silver Spring, MD: National Institute of Drycleaning, 1958.

———. *Modern Textiles.* New York: John Wiley & Sons, 1976.

Madden, Odile, Asuncion Elena Charola, Kim Cullen Cobb, Paula T. DePriest, and Robert J. Koestler, eds. *The Age of Plastic: Ingenuity and Responsibility.* Washington, DC: Smithsonian Institution Scholarly Press, 2017.

Madden, Odile, and Tom Learner. "Preserving Plastics: An Evolving Material, A Maturing Profession." In *Conservation of Plastics,* Getty Conservation Institute newsletter, Spring 2014.

Morgan, John. "A Joint Project on the Conservation of Plastics by the Conservation Unit and the Plastics Historical Society." In Grattan, *Saving the Twentieth Century,* 43–50.

Mossman, Susan. "Plastic in the Science Museum, London: A Curator's View." In Grattan, *Saving the Twentieth Century,* 25–35.

Mossman, Susan, and Marie-Laure Abel. "Testing Treatments to Slow Down the Degradation of Cellulose Acetate." In Keneghan and Egan, *Plastics,* 106–15.

Museums & Galleries NSW. "Deaccession and Disposal in Small Museums." *Sustaining Places.* Sept. 2012. https://sustainingplaces.files.wordpress.com/2012/09/deaccession-and-disposal-in-small-museums.pdf.

Paddock, Katherine Hess. *Textile Fibers and Their Use.* Chicago: J. B. Lippincott, 1931.

Potter, M. D. *Fiber to Fabric: A Textbook on Textiles for the Consumer.* New York: Gregg, 1945.

Preservation of Plastic ARTefacts in Museum Collections. "List of Degradation Terms." *POPART: Preservation Of Plastic ARTifacts in museum collections.* http://popart-highlights.mnhn.fr/wp-content/uploads/3_Collection_survey/1_What_is_the_condition_of_the_collection/List_of_terms.pdf.

———. "What Is the Condition of the Collection?" *POPART: Preservation Of Plastic ARTifacts in museum collections.* http://popart-highlights.mnhn.fr/collection-survey/what-is-the-condition-of-the-collection/index.html.

Price, Arthur, Allen Cohen, and Ingrid Johnson. *J. J. Pizzuto's Fabric Science.* New York: Fairchild, 1999.

Prichard, Sue, and Suzanne Smith. "Taking a Risk: Collecting for the Future." In Keneghan and Egan, *Plastics,* 132–37.

Prytulak, George. "Display and Storage of Museum Objects Containing Cellulose Nitrate." *CCI Notes* 15/3. Canadian Conservation Institute. 1998. https://www.canada.ca/en/conservation-institute/services/conservation-preservation-publications/canadian-conservation-institute-notes/display-storage-objects-cellulose-nitrate.html.

Qian Zhang and Chi-Wai Kan. "A Review of Fusible Interlinings Usage in Garment Manufacture." *Polymers* 10, no. 11 (2018): 1230.

Quye, Anita. "Historical Plastics Come of Age." *Chemistry in Britain* 31, no. 8 (1995): 617–20.

Quye, Anita, and Colin Williamson, eds. *Plastics: Collecting and Conserving.* Edinburgh: NMS, 1999.

Rath, Lois. "Artificial Silk." *Journal of Home Economics* 14, no. 9 (Sept. 1922): 425–29.

Reappraisal and Deaccessioning Development and Review Team, revised by the Technical Subcommittee on Guidelines for Reappraisal and Deaccessioning. "Guidelines for Reappraisal and Deaccessioning [2017]." Society of American Archivists website. Revised May 2017. https://www2.archivists.org/sites/all/files/GuidelinesForReappraisalDeaccessioning_2017.pdf.

Reilly, Julie. "Celluloid Objects: Their Chemistry and Preservation." *Journal of the American Institute for Conservation* 30, no. 2 (Fall 1991): 145–62.

Reuss, Margrit. "Whodunnit? Imitation Jewellery Made from Early Plastics." In Wright, *Ethnographic Beadwork,* 113–16.

Rogerson, Cordelia, and Paul Garside, eds. *The Future of the Twentieth Century: Collecting, Interpreting and Conserving Modern Materials.* London: Archetype, 2005.

Shashoua, Yvonne. "Conservation of Plastics: Is It Possible Today?" In Keneghan and Egan, *Plastics,* 12–19.

Shaw, Merle B., and George W. Bicking. "Rayon as a Paper-Making Material." *Journal of Research* 4, no. 2 (1929): 203–11.

Smith, Betty, and Ira Block. *Textiles in Perspective.* Englewood Cliffs, NJ: Prentice-Hall, 1982.

Steele, Valerie. *Fifty Years of Fashion: New Look to Now.* New Haven: Yale University Press, 2000.

Storms, Lillian. "Paper Textiles." *Journal of Home Economics* 10, no. 10 (Oct. 1918): 451–56.

Stout, Evelyn. *Introduction to Textiles.* New York: John Wiley & Sons, 1962.

Stout, Evelyn, Carol Zillgitt, and Muriel Ferraro. "Effects of Laundering and Drycleaning on Laboratory Performance of Certain Resin-Finished Winter Cottons." *Journal of Home Economics* 49, no. 3 (Mar. 1957): 197–202.

Timar-Balazsy, Agnes, and Dinah Eastop. *Chemical Principles of Textile Conservation.* New York: Routledge, 2011.

Tortora, Phyllis G. *Understanding Textiles.* New York: Macmillan, 1987.

Tortora, Phyllis G., and Robert S. Merkel, *Fairchild's Dictionary of Textiles.* 7th ed. New York: Fairchild, 2003.

ul-Hassan, Waheed. "Polyurethanes History." *Polyurethanes—Foam, Manufacturing Process, Raw Materials, Suppliers.* Feb. 17, 2008. http://urethanestechnology.blogspot.com/2008/02/.

University of Alaska Museum of the North. "Deaccessioning and Disposal." University of Alaska, Museum of the North. https://www.uaf.edu/museum/collections/ethno/policies/deaccessioning/.

van Oosten, Thea, "Preserving Plastic: Challenges in the Conservation of Modern Art Objects." In Madden, Charola, Cobb, DePriest, and Koestler, *Age of Plastic,* 125–39.

Walford, Jonathan. "Paper Dresses." Vintage Fashion Guild website. 2008. https://vintagefashionguild.org/fashion-history/paper-dresses/.

Wilcox, Claire. *A Century of Bags.* Edison: Chartmill Books, 1997.

Wiles, David. "Changes in Polymeric Materials with Time." In Grattan, *Saving the Twentieth Century* 105–11.

Williams, R. Scott. "The Diphenylamine Spot Test for Cellulose Nitrate in Museum Objects." *CCI Notes* 17/2. Canadian Conservation Institute. 1994. https://www.canada.ca/en/conservation-institute/services/conservation-preservation-publications/canadian-conservation-institute-notes/diphenylamine-test-cellulose-nitrate.html.

Wingate, Isabel, ed. *Fairchild's Dictionary of Textiles.* 2nd ed. New York: Fairchild, 1967.

———. *Fairchild's Dictionary of Textiles.* 6th ed. New York: Fairchild, 1979.

———. *Textile Fabrics and Their Selection.* New York: Prentice-Hall, 1936.

———. *Textile Fabrics and Their Selection.* 6th ed. Englewood Cliffs, NJ: Prentice-Hall, 1970.

Wingate, Isabel, Karen Gillespie, and Betty Milgrom. *Know Your Merchandise: For Retailers and Consumers.* 4th ed. New York: McGraw-Hill, 1975.

Woolman, Mary Schneck, and Ellen Beers McGowan. *Textiles: A Handbook for the Student and the Consumer.* New York: Macmillan, 1943.

Wright, Margot, ed. *Ethnographic Beadwork: Aspects of Manufacture, Use and Conservation.* London: Archetype, 2001.

Index

Page references in italics refer to illustrations.

acetate garments and accessories, 2–3, 15–18; agitating, 17–18; burning, 15–16; cleaning, 16–17; cleaning, dry, 16–18; cleaning, wet, 16–17; color fading, 16; creases, 16; disperse dyes, 16, 18, 24; dust covers, 17; exhibiting, 16–17; flattening, 16, 18; folding, 17; FTC categorization, 15; fume fading, 16–18; glaze marks, 16–17; handling, 16–17; identification, 15; light, 17–18; microscopic examination of, 15; military use, 15; pressing, 16; solubility, 15; steaming, 17–18; storing, 16–17; strength, 15–16; velvets, 15–18; wet, 16
acetic acid, 48, 95
acetone, 1, 27, 48, 96
Acrilan, 25
acrylic garments and accessories, 23, 25–27; burning, 25; cleaning, 26–27; cleaning, dry, 26; cleaning, wet, 26; dimensional stability, 26; elongation, 26; exhibiting, 26–27; heat-molded dresses, 25; identification, 25; knitted sweater, 26, 27; microscopic examination, 25; solubility, 25; steaming, 26; storing, 26
adhered seams, hems, and pleats, 71–72; adhesive failure, 71–72; cleaning, 71–72; cleaning, dry, 71–72; cleaning, wet, 71–72;

exhibiting, 71; handling, 71; identification, 71; staining, 71–72; steaming, 71; storing, 71; testing, 71
adhesives, 57–75; adhered seams, hems, and pleats, 71–72; bonded and laminated fabrics, 60–62; bonded ornamentation, 57–60; bonded-wool shoulder pads, 72–75; Chem Stitch fabrics, 65–67; flocked fabrics, 67–70; fusible interfacings and interlinings, 62–65; purpose, 57; quilted linings, 72–75
American Institute of Launderers, 1
Arachne, 35
Araknit, 35
Aralac, 21
Avisco rayon, 12
azlon, 21

Bayer, Otto, 89
Bemberg, 10
B. F. Goodrich, 50
Big Ben jelly-style blue sandals, 53
bonded and laminated fabrics, 60–62; blistering, 62; bonded skiwear fabrics, 60, 62; cleaning, 60–62; cleaning, dry, 60–62; cleaning, wet, 62; delaminated fabrics, 60; exhibiting, 60–61; foam, 60–62; folding, 61; handling, 61; identification, 60; interface, 61; jersey, 60; tricot, 60, 62; separation, 60–62; shrinkage, 60–61; small-dot application patterns, 60; steaming,

61; stiffening, 61; storing, 60–61; testing, 61
bonded ornamentation, 57–60; aging, 58; agitating, 59; beads, 60; buttons, 60; cleaning, dry, 60; cleaning, wet, 58; cork trim, 59; exhibiting, 58–59; felt cut-outs, 57, 59; folding, 59; glitter, 59–60; glued-on rhinestones, 58; handling, 59; leather and suede trim, 59; sequins, 59; steaming, 59; storing, 58, 59; velvet trim, 59
bonded-wool quilted linings, 3, 72–75; adhesive failure, 73, 75; cleaning, 73–75; cleaning, dry, 72, 74; cleaning, wet, 74; degradation, 73, 74; exhibiting, 73–75; handling, 74–75; identification, 73; interlining, 3, 73; jacket lining, 73, 74; neoprene, 72–75; odor, 73; staining, 75; steaming, 74; stiffening, 75; storing, 73–75
bonded-wool shoulder pads, 3, 72–75; adhesive failure, 73, 75; cleaning, 73–75; cleaning, dry, 72, 74; cleaning, wet, 74; color change, 73, 75; degradation, 73, 74; exhibiting, 73–75; handling, 74–75; identification, 73; interlining, 3, 73; jacket, 75; neoprene, 72–75; odor, 73; staining, 75; steaming, 74; stiffening, 75; storing, 73–75

camphor, 90–91
Cardin, Pierre, 25
Cardine, 25